MORE PROFIT FROM YOUR PC

MORE PROFIT FROM YOUR PC

How to turn your PC into an Investment Powerhouse

David Linton

B. T. BATSFORD LTD · LONDON

Batsford Business Online: www.batsford.com

First published 1996
Second impression 1997
This edition 1998
© David Linton

Published by B T Batsford Ltd,
583 Fulham Road,
London SW6 5BY

Batsford Business Online: www.batsford.com

ISBN 0 7134 8388 1

A CIP catalogue record for this book is available from
The British Library

Printed by:
Redwood Books
Kennet House
Kennet Way
Trowbridge
Wiltshire, BA14 8RN

Contents

To Johnny and Sarah, two great friends who have influenced me enormously.

Acknowledgements

Profit from your PC was derived from material I had produced and discovered over several years and brought together while on holiday in the Caribbean. This follow-up book was mainly produced in another beautiful part of the world, Cornwall, England. This stunning area reminds me of where I was brought up outside Melbourne in Australia. The Cornish people are delightful and I am particularly grateful to Fyonah Hastings and her family for providing me with an idyllic retreat in which to focus on this book. Fy is one of a number of people I have come to know at the Alma Tavern, opposite Updata House. This humble venue has also provided us at Updata with an informal environment in which to meet our customers and understand them as investors. Thanks are due to all the staff there who run around us.

I am grateful to a number of people who took the trouble to provide me with feedback in the *Profit from your PC* Reader Survey, which is covered in the back of this book.

As I expected, I failed to acknowledge someone in the last book. Thanks are due to Lisa Granger, an accomplished journalist and dear friend who has read through my scribblings on numerous occasions. Patrick Littlehales at European Stockbrokers has been very helpful over a number of years and has looked after a number of Updata customers. He is a rare breed of broker: calm, collected and focused on cutting losses and running with profits. He has been a useful sounding board throughout the production of this book. The 'rabbit's teeth' in Chapter 4 are his. Kate Pope helped advise on many aspects of producing a second book.

Once again, thanks to all staff at Updata who really got behind me in bringing yet another project to fruition. The enthusiasm of the team to be the best is outstanding and a joy to be part of. In the early days I used to visit customers up and down the country to help them get up and running. I was delighted to find, while working on this book in the office one Saturday, that David from our help desk was gathering what he needed to make a long train journey to assist a stranded customer. This all helps us to understand private investors better.

Particular thanks are due to Stephen Onerhime, Updata's technical mainstay. He has become knowledgeable about markets within the five years he has been at the company and has been helpful on the book. He was described by a number of Updata staff in an internal questionnaire as 'smart, admirable ethic, rarely mistaken judgement, impartial, has a willingness to teach and explain, patient, full of praise and understanding, ability to be logical and objective'. I am truly fortunate to have worked alongside him. He is an incredible colleague.

Thanks to John Winters at Batsford, my new publisher, for embracing the *More Profit from your PC* title and pushing to get this latest impression out.

And finally, thanks to my house mates Johnny and Sarah Robinson. Johnny didn't get a mention in the last book and pointed out to me that I had borrowed one of his ties for the cover picture. He took the cover picture this time to ensure the tie was mine. Thanks. Sarah was a great proof reader and guiding light again, picking up on a number of loose ends and poorly explained concepts.

Preface

More Profit from your PC was first published in 1996 as a follow-up book to the original *Profit from your PC* book produced a year earlier. It has been through two reprints since and I am delighted that my new publisher, BT Batsford, has chosen to re-produce the title in this latest impression. We deliberated over rewriting the book completely and decided, like its predecessor, that it was probably best left alone. On the basis of reader response, it seems people like it as it is and, rather than a rewrite, would probably prefer another follow-on. Stay tuned.

I have been overwhelmed at the general response and feedback I have received from readers of both *Profit from your PC* and *More Profit from your PC*. I was even more surprised to find the press calling me an investment guru along with requests for another book. I have also been amazed that people are asking me to expand into some fairly general areas about investment and even looking for advice on which actual stocks to buy. While I sit in a privileged position to observe markets and investors, I am no investment 'whizz kid'. I am not a 'recognised' professional which, fortunately, precludes me from offering specific investment advice. Secondly, the whole spirit of this and the previous book is that you should be able to do your own homework and beat the 'recognised' professionals a good deal of the time. Consequently, **this book is designed to help you to help yourself**.

I have been extremely fortunate with a large number of Updata customers, including some who have become more involved in the company, and *Profit* readers providing me with guidance and ideas. This book is longer than the first, primarily due to a high number of requests to provide more examples, so please don't be put off by its increased size. It should take less time to get through than a book half its thickness.

My first instinct, in producing *More Profit from your PC*, was to write an updated edition of *Profit*, but I was increasingly persuaded that there was enough material for a whole new title which built on the first book rather than replacing it. *Profit from your PC* is not essential reading as a background to this book. The original book and subsequent feedback is summarised in the first part of this book. Clearly readers of *Profit* will be at an advantage picking up on this new title.

My main reason for writing this book is the realisation that I touched on something that people related to in the last book. I have also found from some readers that I left a few stones unturned. This is my way of dealing with the collection of requests and ideas put forward. I feel a bit like the creator of a follow-up movie, or first album of music that never quite has the impact of the first release. That is partly because when producing the first work, you don't really allow for a sequel. Most of the mileage in the story is spent. It is a culmination of a longer thinking time and a product of a greater desire for excellence. Maybe it is better to go out on a high, than run the risk of a deteriorating performance. I will only know how this book compares with my first via feedback from readers at the addresses given below. If you find this book to be less useful than *Profit from your PC*, I apologise now. If the consensus is such, then I am faced with another double or quits scenario of producing a third book. At least then I will have the benefit of comparison. Your patience in reading this book and any feedback are much appreciated. Thank you.

This book was written using:

1. My faithful Gateway 2000 colour portable computer
2. Microsoft Windows '95
3. Microsoft Word 7 (Word processor)
4. Netscape Navigator, for the Internet Section
5. *Updata Invest** (Graphs pasted into Word in three mouse clicks)

* *Invest* for most graphs, *Updata Analytics* for intra-day graphs and other Updata products for screen shots.

I welcome any correspondence from readers at:

Updata Software (Readers)   Tel: 0181 874 4747
Updata House   Fax: 0181 874 3931
Old York Road
London   Email: Readers@updata.co.uk
                                   Internet: www.updata.co.uk

Introduction

* *

'How do you make a small fortune in stocks and shares?

Start with a big one!' — unknown, disillusioned investor

If you don't have a big fortune to start with you will need something more than a hit and miss strategy. Read on.

In *Profit from your PC,* I based my introduction on a large amount of feedback from a wide audience of private investors. Here I have based the following points on more in-depth feedback from a smaller number of investors, Updata users and a handful of private client stockbrokers.

Where most investors still go wrong

Profit readers consistently identified the most important message of the book to be:

1. **Cut losses**

2. **Cut losses**

3. **Cut losses**

4. **Let profits run**

Many pointed out the dichotomy that a book about profit had an over-riding message to focus on losses. Nothing has changed. The inability to cut losses is still the private investor's biggest enemy.

While it seems that this message has reached people loud and clear, many have indicated that they have been less good at putting it into practice. Investors have watched their stop-losses being breached before their eyes and reverted back to their old ways of doing nothing.

I can't resist putting my head in the sand

In the middle of 1996, western stockmarkets became extremely volatile. Many experienced market followers began predicting a stockmarket crash. This was the surest sign that it probably wouldn't happen. The unexpected normally happens in markets, a primary reason for their existence. As the Dow Jones index tumbled ten per cent in the first couple of weeks in July, I have to admit to being a little concerned.

What was surprising was that in fairly heavy trading volume for the summer, private client brokers were reporting being very quiet. Daily trading volume on the London Stock Exchange is normally around 80% institutional. Over this period, I would suggest it was considerably higher. It seems most active private investors put their heads in the sand. Why? They seemingly watched their share prices sail through their stop-losses and decided to do nothing. Suddenly they froze. The dramatic movement in the market meant it was better to do nothing. We will look at this scenario in more detail shortly. Investors were lucky. Markets bounced back miraculously over the next few weeks. Next time we may not be so lucky.

The institutions beat me to it,
I am too late to do anything

This is a very common complaint among private investors. While there is some validity to this in terms of seconds or even a day or two in response time to news and price movements, it has become an overdone excuse. Investors need to be more adept at seeing the picture unfold. In fact very short term market reactions are frequently overdone, such that there may be an advantage to not being able to react too quickly.

In the case of the recent downturn in the Dow Jones, still the lead indicator for the UK market, there was time to assess what was going on.

I find it difficult to put dramatic moves into context

The warning signs came when the Dow fell through a medium term support level. This is illustrated in the chart on page 13. The key price levels are shown, where the trend lines finish on the right-hand scale. These change with time due to the slope of the trends, but it is very useful to have a good idea of these levels. They provide an indication of the extent of the downside potential .

Source: Updata

The graph and trend lines above show the following key levels on the Dow Jones:

- 5800, the level it needs to break to carry on rising
- 5700, the level it needs to stay above to maintain the medium term trend
- 5335, where it needs to stay above for clear sideways movement
- 5200, the absolute lower limit for sideways movement
- 5100, the lower limit of a slow downward trend
- 4150, below this level sees the end of a very long bull run

The falls in the market provided a series of new support levels. Before this the market was much harder to read, with the only clear support at 4150. The same can be done for the FT-SE 100 index, which in September 1996 was hitting all time highs.

My gut feel for what is happening is often wrong

'Gut feeling' and 'gut reaction' are two different things and are not to be confused. Gut reactions are arrived at hastily without considering the facts, while gut feelings are based on experience and your better judgement.

Many investors arrive at their gut feel for what is happening and going to happen before considering the possibilities. It is normally a case of simple logic. Many people think the market will either go up or down. This is like betting on red or black. Markets are not always a two way bet and the complex issues that can drive price means there are many more horses to back. For example, looking at the Dow Jones graph on page 13, there are three possible scenarios.

1.   The market breaks into new ground and continues to rise.

2.   The market continues to trade sideways for some time as a slow form of consolidation against the recent strong rise over eighteen months.

3.   The market falls sharply as a fast form of consolidation against the recent strong rise over eighteen months.

You may even consider splitting each scenario further, such as rising fast and rising slowly. Once you have considered the possibilities, it becomes much easier to arrive at what you believe to be the most likely scenario. You may decide having considered these options that (1) is extremely unlikely and that you favour (2) over (3). But if, say, scenario (3) begins to unfold, **you may be prepared to accept your gut feel was wrong.**

This is probably the biggest single advantage of continual technical assessment over analysis based on fundamentals. It is much easier to be reactive and adapt accordingly.

This exercise can be done over a number of different time periods to formulate short, medium and long term views.

I still have trouble choosing the right stocks

In *Profit from your PC*, we identified four types of stock to buy:

1.   Recovery situations – reversals from a long term trend

2.   Breakouts – dramatic movements from a narrowing trading range

3.   Trending Stocks – shares already behaving in a clear upward trend

4.   Character Changes – a change in behaviour

A number of readers have expressed difficulties in spotting these types of share, so we will cover a new selection of examples in the next section.

The key is to focus your skills on one or two of these types of pattern.

I have trouble spotting the beginning and end of trends

The end of trends should be fairly straightforward. A fall through a support line is quite clear. The difficulty seems to be knowing where exactly to draw the trend line. If you are unable to do this, stop-loss ultimately amounts to much the same thing. A breach of the stop-loss often occurs where the breakdown through the trend occurs.

Identifying the beginning of a trend is also fairly straightforward. New trends will normally develop off a change in behaviour. For example a recovery or a breakout situation will signal the beginnings of a new trend as shown below:

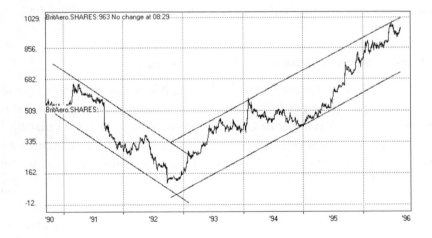

Source: Updata

In this recovery, the trend channels begin and end at the trough.

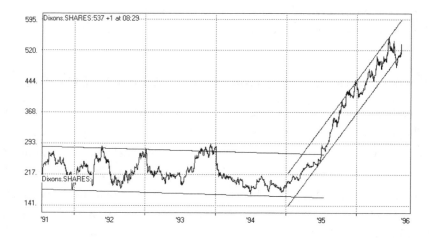

Source: Updata

In this breakout, the new trend started as the old sideways trend channel finished.

I am not sure which stop-loss I should use

In *Profit from your PC*, we identified that the best stop-loss was the one that had worked well historically on the particular share being monitored. We will look at this again in the next section. A number of Updata customers have identified that they actually use two stop-losses. One to serve as a warning and signal to be on guard for a breach, the other for the actual sell signal. This leads to this type of example shown on page 17.

> "My stop-losses have taken me out of
> everything, what do I do?
> Be grateful!"

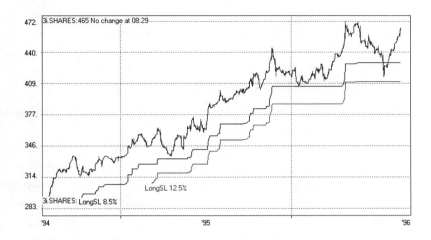

Source: Updata

My stop-losses have taken me out of everything, what do I do?

Be grateful would be my first response. Many investors panic about not being in the market. My view is the opportunities always present themselves. For those who feel they must be fully invested, the logical answer is to find stocks that haven't fallen through their stop-losses. Have a look at the graph below:

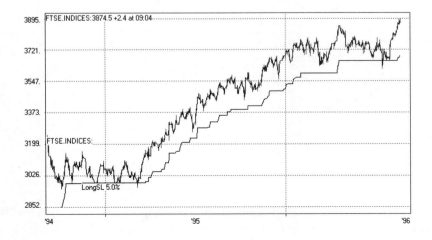

Source: Updata

While the FT-SE index shown on page 17 breached a 5% stop-loss for the first time in two years, over one third of the constituent stocks did not. Even though the market looked bad there were some interesting buying opportunities about.

The market looks bad, I am put off investing

While it is true that one shouldn't buck the market, it is also true that investors should be trying to out-perform the market at all times.

We, at Updata, are always surprised to see a strong improvement in investment software sales when the stockmarket rallies. When nearly everything is going up investors tend to do quite well even with a hit or miss strategy. It is when uncertainty reigns or we see the market moving sideways, that investment software tools come into their own. At these times, investments need closer monitoring, a task for which personal computers are ideally suited. Suddenly not having the information and the tools to analyse it, means that you feel a few steps behind rather than on top of your investments.

Often the best stocks just keep on being the best. Investors are surprised that a buy high and sell higher strategy can actually work. If you don't believe this just look at the leaders and laggards tables on pages 18 - 20.

1	Std Chtd	74.94	27	SKlineB	22.48	53	Pearson	9.52	76	Reckitt	-3.87
2	Dixons	67.29	28	TI Grp	22.1	54	M & S	9.43	77	Guinness	-4.36
3	BSkyB	60.94	29	Utd News	21.94	55	Scot & N	8.96	78	Corn Uni	-4.37
4	BritAero	50.94	30	Blue Cir	20.06	56	RTZ	8.32	79	RMC Grp	-4.45
5	Argos	50.4	31	R-Royce	20	57	LASMO	7.26	80	Cable&W	-5.34
6	Next	41.55	32	Br Air	19.13	58	Burmah	7.16	81	BAA	-5.63
7	Burton	40.71	33	Reed Int	19.06	59	For&Col	7.14	82	Pilk'ton	-5.8
8	Rentokil	40.27	34	3i	18.32	60	Gen Acc	6.23	83	BT	-6.03
9	Kingfish	38.08	35	Glaxo	17.05	61	Williams	5.52	84	Severn T	-6.59
10	Siebe	36.47	36	Wolseley	15.99	62	GUS	5.09	85	Courtald	-7.38
11	Enterprs	35	37	Railtrack	15.81	63	Rank	4.36	86	Tesco	-8.06
12	Zeneca	34.68	38	Ladbroke	15.01	64	Tomkins	3.67	87	Scot Pwr	-9.04
13	GKN	33.29	39	Royal & S	14.99	65	Unilever	3.44	88	Southern	-10.04
14	Legal &G	33.03	40	Royal Bk	14.19	66	BOC	2.94	89	P&O dfd	-10.63
15	Granada	32.09	41	GRE	13.78	67	Bnk Scot	2.44	90	Vodafone	-10.78
16	Smithsl	32.01	42	Whitbred	13.17	68	Cadbury	1.91	91	Nat Grd	-13.78
17	HSBC $	31.67	43	NatWest	13.07	69	EMI	1.51	92	PowerGen	-14.45
18	BP	29.48	44	Grand Mt	12.86	70=	Ald Domeq	0	93	Sainsbry	-15.32
19	Reuters	28.18	45	Boots	11.86	70=	ICI	0	94	Orange	-17.52
20	Shell	28.13	46	Asda Grp	11.85	70=	Schrodr	0	95	BAT Inds	-18.94
21	Barclays	27.79	47	AB Foods	11.57	70=	Utd Utils	0	96	NatPower	-22.52
22	LloyTSB	26.81	48	Redland	10.97	71	Tate & L	-0.85	97	BTR	-25.74
23	ThornEMI	26.25	49	Abbey Nt	10.66	72	Br Steel	-1.1	98	Hanson	-28.02
24	Pru Corp	25.66	50	Carlton	9.94	73	ThamesWtr	-1.45	99	Br Gas	-28.94
25	GEC	24.8	51	FTSE	9.75	74	Smith &N	-1.53			
26	Bass	23.85	52	Land Sec	9.64	75	Safeway	-2.85			

Source: Updata

The FT-SE 100 ranked by the 12 month percentage change shows that over two thirds of the stocks went up, with half out-performing the Index, a quarter out-performing it more than two fold and ten percent more than four fold.

#			#			#			#		
1	BSkyB	37.34	26	Asda Grp	11.32	52	Br Steel	3.45	76	GUS	-3.22
2	Enterprs	34.29	27	Blue Cir	11.14	53	Vodafone	3	77	For&Col	-4.26
3	Kingfish	26.92	28	Ladbroke	9.73	54	Williams	2.99	78	Com Uni	-4.37
4	Argos	25.62	29	3i	9.67	55	GEC	2.5	79	Pru Corp	-4.48
5	GKN	22.75	30	Reed Int	9.38	56	Abbey Nt	2.21	80	NatWest	-4.8
6	Zeneca	20.31	31	Land Sec	9.28	57	Gen Acc	1.84	81	BOC	-4.99
7	Dixons	19.6	32	Reuters	8.32	58	Utd Utils	1.8	82	Cadbury	-5.4
8	BP	19.28	33	Smithsl	7.99	59	Royal & S	1.79	83	Tomkins	-5.58
9	Granada	18.5	34	Guinness	7.93	60	EMI	1.51	84	PowerGen	-5.71
10	Std Chtd	17.69	35	Schrodr	7.84	61=	Smith &N	1.31	85	Severn T	-7.32
11	Rentokil	17.09	36	HSBC $	7.7	61=	ThamesWtr	1.31	86	Pilk'ton	-7.58
12	M & S	16.27	37	Grand Mt	7	62	Scot & N	0.9	87	Bnk Scot	-9.03
13	Next	16.04	38	Unilever	6.6	63	Rank	0.42	88	ICI	-9.75
14	Carlton	15.9	39	Boots	6.22	64	Reckitt	0.15	89	Cable&W	-10.92
15	Railtrack	15.81	40	R-Royce	5.21	65	Legal &G	0.14	90	Royal Bk	-11.05
16	Barclays	14.95	41	RTZ	4.9	66=	Ald Domeq	0	91	Nat Grd	-11.79
17	Siebe	13.87	42	Br Air	4.39	66=	BT	0	92	Br Gas	-13.87
18	Burton	13.04	43	LASMO	4.35	67	Courtald	-0.68	93	Hanson	-15.96
19	LloyTSB	12.15	44	Redland	4.32	68	Whitbred	-0.7	94	NatPower	-17.14
20	TI Grp	12.13	45	AB Foods	4.11	69	Glaxo	-0.97	95	Orange	-17.52
21=	Bass	11.99	46	RMC Grp	3.75	70	Burmah	-1.04	96	Southern	-19.23
21=	Safeway	11.99	47	Sainsbry	3.65	71	BAA	-1.82	97	Scot Pwr	-19.25
22	BritAero	11.98	48	GRE	3.64	72	P&O dfd	-1.91	98	BTR	-21.09
23	Shell	11.87	49	FTSE	3.6	73	Wolseley	-2.14	99	BAT Inds	-25.82
24	ThornEMI	11.85	50	Utd News	3.51	74	Pearson	-2.91			
25	Tesco	11.59	51	SKlineB	3.49	75	Tate & L	-3.13			

Source: Updata

A six monthly leaders, again shows more than half out-performing the index with 10% out-performing by five times.

#			#			#			#		
1	BSkyB	21.51	26	Glaxo	6.85	51	Burmah	0.87	76	Nat Grd	-2.55
2	Barclays	18.06	27	Abbey Nt	6.74	52	Carlton	0.86	77	Safeway	-2.57
3	Br Gas	17.48	28	Kingfish	6.62	53	Tomkins	0.79	78	Reckitt	-2.76
4	HSBC $	16.32	29	Utd Utils	5.88	54	RMC Grp	0.57	79	Reuters	-2.96
5	Railtrack	15.81	30	Land Sec	5.34	55	Pilk'ton	0.52	80	P&O dfd	-3.21
6	Std Chtd	15.02	31	Granada	5.32	56	TI Grp	0.37	81	RTZ	-3.22
7	LloyTSB	14.29	32	Tesco	5.12	57	Gen Acc	0.3	82	Smith &N	-3.73
8	SKlineB	13.3	33	Williams	4.88	58	Courtald	0.23	83	Bnk Scot	-3.82
9	BT	11.81	34	Unilever	4.61	59=	Ald Domeq	0	84	Pearson	-4.3
10	Zeneca	10.28	35	Reed Int	4.19	59=	For&Col	0	85	GRE	-4.48
11	BP	9.22	36	Bass	4.14	60	Next	-0.18	86	BOC	-5.71
12	Ladbroke	9.14	37	Argos	3.99	61	3i	-0.21	87	Royal & S	-6.78
13	NatWest	8.87	38	Sainsbry	3.65	62	Wolseley	-0.22	88	Rank	-7.17
14	Blue Cir	8.66	39	Schrodr	3.54	63	Rentokil	-0.24	89	Br Air	-7.6
15=	Dixons	8.48	40	FTSE	3.4	64	Asda Grp	-0.42	90	Utd News	-8.25
15=	GEC	8.48	41	Pru Corp	2.9	65	PowerGen	-0.78	91	Cable&W	-8.52
16	Enterprs	8.46	42	Guinness	2.77	66	Scot & N	-0.89	92	ICI	-8.59
17	BritAero	8.45	43	Boots	2.76	67	ThamesWtr	-1.09	93	Southern	-10.99
18	Cadbury	8.09	44	GKN	2.71	68	R-Royce	-1.11	94	Scot Pwr	-11.18
19	Severn T	7.99	45=	Br Steel	1.98	69	Whitbred	-1.66	95	BTR	-11.87
20	M & S	7.76	45=	Legal &G	1.98	70	Burton	-1.97	96	BAT Inds	-14.74
21	Redland	7.41	46	Smithsl	1.67	71	GUS	-2.07	97	Hanson	-17.06
22	Siebe	7.28	47	EMI	1.51	72	Com Uni	-2.31	98	Orange	-19.42
23	LASMO	7.26	48	Shell	1.38	73	BAA	-2.41	99	NatPower	-21.39
24	Grand Mt	7.24	49	Tate & L	1.31	74	Vodafone	-2.44			
25	AB Foods	6.86	50	ThornEMI	1.07	75	Royal Bk	-2.46			

Source: Updata

Over three months – still high levels of out-performance

#			#			#			#		
1	Railtrack	19.14	27	GRE	7.56	51	Bass	4.33	75	Pilk'ton	1.56
2	Barclays	14.73	28	Std Chtd	7.55	52	Courtald	4.28	76	EMI	1.51
3	BSkyB	14.17	29	Abbey Nt	7.5	53	GEC	4.14	77	AB Foods	1.5
4	Grand Mt	11.53	30	Br Steel	7.46	54	Legal &G	4.04	78	Com Uni	1.11
5	HSBC $	11.41	31	Royal & S	7.26	55	Asda Grp	3.74	79	RMC Grp	1.06
6	Tesco	10.79	32	ThornEMI	7.16	56	Safeway	3.49	80	Nat Grd	0.88
7	Zeneca	10.28	33	Utd Utils	6.46	57	P&O dfd	3.43	81	Carlton	0.64
8	Ladbroke	10.03	34	BTR	6.32	58	Wolseley	3.39	82	TI Grp	0.56
9	Severn T	9.78	35	Burmah	6.29	59	NatPower	3.31	83	Pru Corp	0.47
10	Boots	9.44	36	PowerGen	6.22	60	Glaxo	3.25	84	Whitbred	0.14
11	3i	9.41	37=	GUS	6.1	61	Reckitt	3.24	85=	Ald Domeq	0
12	Land Sec	9.28	37=	Next	6.1	62	Cadbury	3.04	85=	R-Royce	0
13	LloyTSB	9.09	38	Royal Bk	6.08	63	Shell	3.03	86	ICI	-0.06
14	NatWest	9.05	39	Schrodr	5.93	64=	Williams	2.99	87	Siebe	-0.22
15	Kingfish	8.55	40	Enterprs	5.88	64=	Guinness	2.99	88	Hanson	-0.32
16	Dixons	8.48	41	BT	5.65	65	Orange	2.93	89	Cable&W	-1.21
17	Vodafone	8.35	42	FTSE	5.25	66	Scot & N	2.92	90	Burton	-1.48
18	Sainsbry	8.3	43	Unilever	5.12	67	M & S	2.82	91	BAA	-2.02
19	Blue Cir	8.06	44	Pearson	5.04	68	Rentokil	2.62	92	ThamesWtr	-2.51
20	Granada	7.85	45	For&Col	5	69	Southern	2.44	93	Tomkins	-2.68
21	RTZ	7.84	46	LASMO	4.92	70=	Redland	2.35	94	Scot Pwr	-3.21
22	SKlineB	7.78	47	Reed Int	4.57	70=	Rank	2.35	95	BOC	-4.27
23	Bnk Scot	7.69	48	Gen Acc	4.56	71	BritAero	2.01	96	Smith &N	-5.61
24	BP	7.63	49=	Smithsl	4.43	72	Tate & L	1.86	97	BAT Inds	-12.02
25	Utd News	7.62	49=	Argos	4.43	73	GKN	1.79			
26	Br Gas	7.61	50	Reuters	4.35	74	Br Air	1.65			

Source: Updata

Over one month – with the bulk of stocks ahead, will these new leaders be the star performers over the coming year?

Company accounts are far more useful than technical analysis

Over the years I have had a number of seasoned investors dismiss the simple graphing techniques I have presented as anything ranging from interesting to complete baloney. 'You can't beat traditional fundamental analysis' has been the response. Fundamental analysis requires the investor to build an understanding of a company mainly through analysing the company's accounts and prospects. There are two key points here, **1) the year end position has normally been assessed by the market and is therefore already reflected in the share price, 2) can the data be trusted anyway?**

Picking up on the second point. In 1992, Terry Smith, an analyst and Head of UK Company Research with UBS Phillips & Drew, produced a book called *Accounting for Growth – stripping the camouflage from company accounts*. He moved on from UBS and a number of renowned city figures, including key representatives of the accounting industry, tried to get the book banned. In his book he identified that a large number of highly regarded UK companies were in effect 'cooking the books'. The list of companies mentioned in the book's index reads like a list of top UK companies. Smith showed that, while these practices were within recommended accounting guidelines, many companies were using 'tricks of the trade' in presenting their financial position. These accounting areas included:

1. Acquisition Accounting

2. Sales and Disposals

3. Deferred Consideration

4. Extraordinary Items

5. Cash Flow Accounting

6. Contingent Liabilities

7. Capitalisation of Costs

8. Brand Accounting

9. Changes in Depreciation Policy

10. Transfer from Current to Fixed Assets

11. Currency Mismatching

12. Pension Fund Accounting

13. Goodwill

14. Deferred Tax

Some people will appreciate this subject area more than others, but it doesn't take much to see the scope for a distorted picture with the number of variables involved.

Investors beware! The accounting minefield and the pitfalls of taking company accounts as gospel could be very costly. Smith produced a 'Blob Guide' for companies utilising 'accounting tricks' under any one of the above headings. One top UK company, who shall remain nameless (I'm not as brave as Smith), was found to have used ten such tricks in its reporting. Many more household names were found to have used a handful.

Smith's techniques were nothing short of miraculous for identifying companies where trouble lay ahead. The problem is that most private investors would find this level of research to be fairly laborious and difficult to carry out in a methodical manner.

Having looked at an array of fundamental techniques over the years, I always find myself returning to the share price history, for really understanding what is going on. Fundamental analysis has not really lent itself to the PC environment over the past few years. However, there have been two major advances in this arena:

1. Powerful PCs are now capable of searching, analysing and processing text data

2. This data is starting to become readily available over the Internet

Hence, fundamentals data is covered in Part 3 of this book.

Points to remember

1. **Cut Losses**

2. **Cut Losses**

3. **Cut Losses**

4. **Let Profits Run**

Some new points

1. Use stop-losses more rigidly

2. Don't put your head in the sand

3. Don't think the professionals have beaten you to it

4. Put dramatic moves into context quickly to remove uncertainty

5. Look at likely scenarios before establishing your gut feel

6. Focus on types of stock to choose

7. Practise spotting the beginning and end of trends

8. Establish which stop-losses work best

9. Don't take company accounts as gospel, they can be a minefield

PART ONE

Building on
Profit from your PC

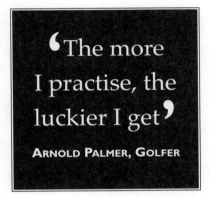

‘The more
I practise, the
luckier I get’
ARNOLD PALMER, GOLFER

CHAPTER ONE

Recapping on
Profit from your PC

● ●

This chapter is essentially a summary of the main points from each of the chapters in *Profit from your PC*. It assists those who wish to refer back and serves as a foundation for those who don't.

The key points that came out of the introduction of *Profit from your PC* were:

1. **Cut losses**
2. **Cut losses**
3. **Cut losses**
4. **Let profits run**

5. Discard useless information
6. Look for information the crowd misses
7. Take a contrary view
8. Never take a tip
9. Sell stocks that are falling
10. Buy stocks that are rising
11. Buy a computer and the right software
12. Get a methodical system in place

The points raised in the introduction of this book have come to the forefront since.

Chapter 1 – A Methodical Approach

Fundamentals versus charting

Fundamentals are less good at assessing the short term. If a price line fails to move in a predicted direction, the fundamental analysis needs to be completely revised while the chart is constantly revising itself.

Technical factors often account for 100% of one day's trading movement. There are exceptions such as when there is a dramatic news item. Over a week a price line's movement is still mainly technical. After a few months movement is half technical and half fundamental. Over six months fundamentals have become more important and after a year it is nearly all fundamentals.

It is harder to act according to price changes using fundamentals and difficult to know the extent of the effect.

Investors should endeavour to place themselves somewhere between these two camps. Based on the above, you should be:

Fundamentals – Long Term
Technical – Short Term

I would favour a position nearer the technical camp as it lends itself more readily to the methodical approach and PC based investment.

Price versus value

'The graph represents all the information that everyone in the market already knows about that particular stock.'

'Markets will tell you the price of everything and the value of nothing.' Most of us relate to this adage as we frequently see the stocks we buy, keep falling and the ones we sell, keep rising. The harsh reality is that most securities are rarely at or near their real value. Nearly all stocks spend most of their time being either overbought or oversold.

The market spends ninety per cent of its time thinking about where it will go and ten per cent of its time getting there. The whole *raison d'être* of the market is uncertainty. Price almost never reflects value as a result of this. Looking for the extremes of over and under-value is where the fun starts.

Rumour

One of the greatest investment stories of all time is that of Nathan Rothschild, founder of one of the richest families in the world. In July, 1815, he got advance word via carrier pigeon of Wellington's victory over Napoleon at Waterloo. His understanding of how markets work told him that the London stockmarket would react strongly to the news.

Rothschild's understanding of crowd behaviour went much further than most, enabling him to increase his upside substantially. Rather than buying, he instructed his sons to go into the market and sell. When investors saw the Rothschilds selling, they panicked and the market crashed. Once prices had hit rock bottom, the Rothschilds started buying heavily. When news reached London of a British victory, stock prices soared. Rothschild made over a million pounds.

Some readers may have seen a similar scenario in the film 'Trading Places', with Eddie Murphy dealing in frozen orange juice futures.

Stranger things have happened. The Tokyo stockmarket once had more than $5 billion wiped off its value in a couple of minutes after news of a virtually unknown UK pop star, Lonnie Donegan, having had a heart attack. This wasn't anything to do with any Japanese cult following of the singer. It came about because, to the Japanese, Ronald Reagan sounded the same.

The key point is that markets are very driven in the short term by rumours of takeovers, companies in trouble, you name it, death, all sorts of things. It is interesting that crowds en masse, in essence the market, often over-react to such rumour. Most successful investors take a contrary view. If it is obvious, it is obviously wrong.

Chapter 2 – Buying a Computer

Advising on buying a computer is not easy. People ask us, at Updata, every day of the week. Prices and specifications are changing all the time. You need to take the plunge sooner or later. Some general guidelines are offered in Chapter 11 of this book.

Chapter 3 – Getting Data

There are a number of ways to get data into your PC. The main types are as follows:

1. Manual Entry
2. TV and Satellite Broadcast
3. Modem – On-line services

These are also covered further in Chapter 11 and the Internet section in Part Three of this book.

Chapter 4 – The Internet

In *Profit from your PC* I felt I was going out on a limb dedicating a whole chapter to the Internet as well as producing an Internet directory. The Internet has now become so central to computing that it is covered by a whole section in this book.

Chapter 5 – Software

Software is expanded in Chapter 11 of this book under the following headings:

1. Operating Systems
2. Word processors, Spreadsheets and databases
3. Investment Software

Chapters 6 & 7 – Basic Technical Analysis and Using Technical Indicators

If you don't already have an approach that works, or want a better one, simple technical analysis will probably be central to your strategy of using a computer for investing. Technical analysis, often known as 'charting', is ideally suited to PC based investment. I prefer the word graphing because I believe the following:

- The graph gives you 90% of the picture

- Understanding the trends gives a further 9%

- Other forms of technical analysis give you the rest and often serve as confirmation

This tends to disappoint the increasing numbers of technical analysts, but the fact is it is much better kept simple. We will cover more sophisticated analysis in this book, but here we will recap on the basics.

Graphs have two main functions:

1. Presentation of historical performance and the latest price changes at a glance.

2. The ability to analyse this information in order to make investment decisions.

A picture of the historic price movement allows the mind to assimilate the information more quickly than a list of tabulated figures and any major price change will be noticed immediately.

The graph represents everything that everyone in the market already knows about the stock. If it is not in the graph, you have a very remote chance of knowing it anyway. Investors may be better studying the effect rather than identifying the cause. It is our obsession with diagnosis that often wastes our time. Patients like to know what is wrong with them more than what will make them better. Do we need to know the reasons why a stock is under or over-valued?

In *Profit from your PC*, we covered the following main areas in the chapters on The Basics of Technical Analysis and Using Technical Indicators:

- Trends

- Cycles

- Overlays

- Averages

- Stop-losses

In *More Profit from your PC* we build on each topic summarised with dedicated chapters. This should help those using each of these techniques as an easier reference to refer back to.

Let's recap briefly on the indicators that were covered. Readers who have not read *Profit from your PC* should be able to pick up on these ideas without too much difficulty. Chapter 9 of this book also looks at the example graphs used in the last book and how they have changed.

Trends

Trends were summarised as follows:

Buy Signals

1. If a 'price line' penetrates upwards through the resistance level of a downward trend channel by a few per cent or more, the trend can be considered to be broken, indicating a price reversal. An upward trend channel should now start to form.

2. If the penetration is upward through an upward trend channel, this indicates that the price line is in new territory. The most likely scenarios are that either the trend channel will become dramatically steeper or the resistance line will become a new level of support.

Sell Signals

1. If a 'price line' penetrates downwards through the support level of an upward trend channel by a few per cent or more the trend can be considered to be broken, signifying a price reversal. A downward trend channel should now start to form.

2. If the penetration is downward through a downward trend channel this indicates that the price line is in new territory and the support line is likely to become a new level of resistance.

The three main tools we looked at were:

    1. Centre lines
    2. Trend channels
    3. Trend lines

The following three graphs are respective examples of this.

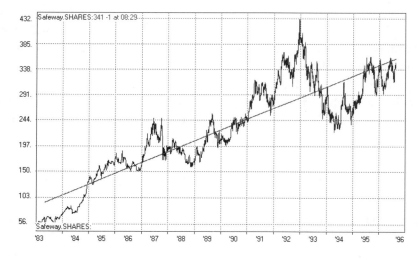

Source: Updata

The centre line used on the graph above is a central regression line, which has been calculated by sampling all the data points and then producing the mean line for all those points. It helps to understand how a share price oscillates between a position of over-value and under-value. Hence, price almost never reflects value.

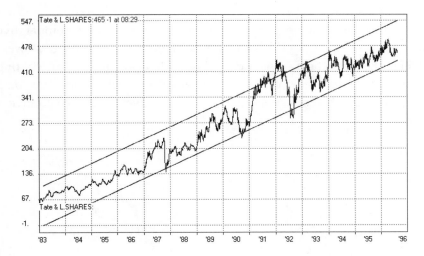

Source: Updata

A trend channel is drawn, by producing two parallel lines, two standard deviations (hence covering 95% of the data), either side of the central regression line. Trend channels are covered in detail in Chapter 3 on 'trends'.

Source: Updata

Trend lines can be drawn manually on graphs in many ways, as above. This is also explained in greater detail under non-period analysis.

Overlays

Overlays are useful for relative performance to the market and comparative analysis with other companies. The main types of overlay we looked at were 're-based', where the graph being overlaid is adjusted to begin at the same starting point and adjusted similarly thereafter, and 'relative' – which divides the data points on the graph by the corresponding ones on the overlay chosen to give a relative graph.

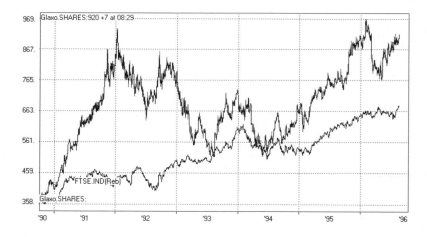

Source: Updata

The graph above shows the FT-SE 100 index rebased. The starting point is adjusted to start at the same point and the subsequent points on the graph are multiplied by that same adjustment factor so that the graphs can be seen on the same axis.

> "The graph represents everything
> that everyone in the market
> already knows."

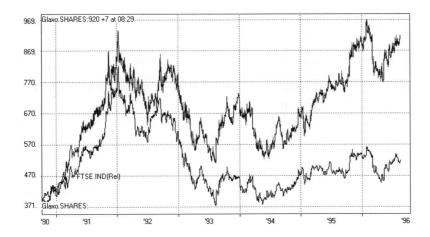

Source: Updata

The FT-SE relative overlay above is produced by dividing every point on the price line by the corresponding point in the FT-SE index and then rebasing the graphs to start at the same point, ie. we are looking at the Glaxo price excluding the effect of the market.

Moving Averages

A moving average smooths the erratic short term fluctuations of the price line and effectively highlights when the price line has diverged from its average. Moving averages tend to 'snake' in a smoothed formation in the general direction of the price movement. This in itself can often be a good indication of cyclical behaviour in a share.

Buy Signals

1. When the price line moves up through its moving average, which is itself rising.

2. When the price line moves down towards its moving average and then bounces off it.

3. When the share price temporarily falls through its moving average, which is still rising, and then bounces back through it.

Sell Signals

1. When the price line is moving down through its moving average which is itself moving down.

2. When the price line moves up towards its moving average, then bounces off it.

3. When the price line temporarily rises through its moving average which itself is falling, then falls back through it.

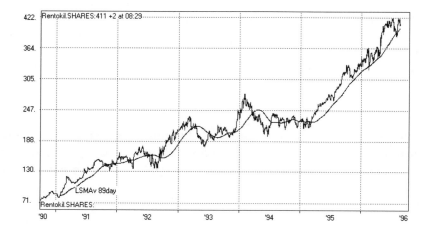

Source: Updata

Rentokil with an 89 day moving average placed on the graph. A fall through the average now would be a signal to sell using this form of analysis.

Stop-losses

Stop-losses are beautifully simple and help take the emotion out of trading. The stop-loss only moves up when the share price exceeds the previous peak.

This helps investors observe the four golden rules of investment:

1. **Cut Losses**
2. **Cut Losses**
3. **Cut Losses**
4. **Let Profits Run**

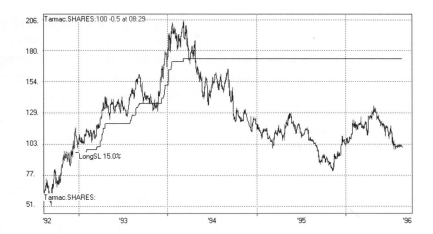

Source: Updata

Avoid this! Let stop-loss help you observe the first three rules, having run with a profit.

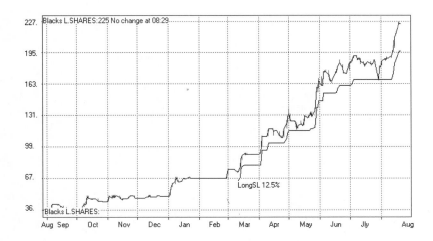

Source: Updata

Ensure this! If you are not sure when the rise in price is over, let stop-loss help you decide.

Chapter 8 – Practice Makes Perfect Profit

This chapter, in *Profit from your PC*, was a walk through of using the stop-loss to play Updata's stockmarket simulation game, Profit for Windows. This book comes with a free voucher for Profit Version 2, an enhanced version that lets you play using overlays and moving averages as well. You can pause the game at any stage to review your progress and print out your results at the end to review your performance.

Chapter 9 – Finding Stocks to Buy

This chapter highlighted four types of share to look for when buying:

1. Recovery situations – reversals from a long term trend

2. Breakouts – dramatic movements from a narrowing trading range

3. Trending Stocks – shares already behaving in a clear upward trend

4. Character Changes – a change in behaviour

All the examples used are reviewed and updated in Chapter 9 of this book. These types of situation are illustrated in the diagram below:

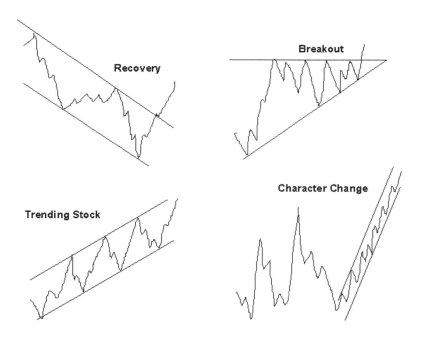

Chapter 10 – Monitoring

Here we looked at monitoring using:

1. Support – the bottom line

2. Stop-losses – to avoid heavy losses

3. Leaders and laggards on a portfolio to see percentage performances

4. Managing portfolios in spreadsheets focusing on annual rate of return

Chapter 11 – When to Sell

Again this looked at support and stop-losses and also worked on the logic that reasons for buying may not have worked out. When to sell highlighted:

1. Reversals through support

2. Taking losses

3. Shares that fall out of bed

4. Recognising you got it wrong – early on – by accepting:

   • a failed recovery

   • a failed breakout

   • getting into a long trend which ends soon after

   • identifying a character change which leads to nothing

Chapter 12 – Getting More Sophisticated

This section covered short term indicators which has been expanded in Chapter 8 in this book. Real time systems and analysis are also covered here under a whole section, Getting More Advanced.

Chapter 13 – Some Examples of a Regular Routine

Short Term Investor – Hold for Days, Weeks – Daily Routine
Medium Term Investor – Hold for Weeks, Months – Weekly Routine
Long Term – Hold for Months, Years – Monthly Routine

A Structured Analysis Routine

1. Analyse the market first.

2. Next, look at any price line and try to spot a trend.

3. Try to identify the likely direction of the price line in the short term.

   - If it has just bounced off resistance or support then it will be towards the other extreme. Determine the price level of this extreme.

   - The best signal is given by a breakout where a trend line has clearly been breached. The price line is moving into new territory.

4. Try to identify cycles to estimate period lengths of the price line.

5. Use overlays to compare the price line with other price lines.

Optional

6. Use moving averages of the period estimated on the price line and look at intersections between them.

7. Use two moving averages preferably of the two periods you have identified. Look for 'crosses'. If no clear signals try fibonacci numbers.

8. Once you feel you can visualise step 6 try using OBOS. Be prepared to go back and draw your interpretation using the moving average.

9. Step 7 can be replaced by using MACD when you feel you have mastered it. Checking signals using the two moving averages is highly recommended.

10. Look at momentum and get a feel for whether the price line is running out of steam or gathering pace.

11. RSI will tell you how strong a price line is relative to the period length selected. Again you are looking for this indicator being in overbought or oversold regions. Remember to compare RSI to price line behaviour looking for previous confirmation of signals.

12. If a price line is beautifully cyclical try using the stochastic function.

Consult the correct interpretations of the indicator being used, including short lists of buy and sell signals, whenever you are in any doubt.

What not to do

The most important point is not to be guided by your emotions, especially fear and greed.

1. Don't decide on whether to buy, sell, or hold until you have completed the analysis, otherwise it will only confirm what you feel.

2. Don't be afraid to accept that you cannot determine what will happen. When in doubt do nowt if you are out. If you are in and in doubt, get out.

3. Adhere to stop-loss rigidly. Protect profits by moving stop-loss up with rises. Protect against losses such that if you are down from the beginning cut your loss and get out.

4. Don't feel you have to trade. Wait for the best signals to come along.

5. Don't predict too far ahead. The further ahead you look the less accurate your prediction is likely to be.

6. Don't anticipate price reversals and breakouts. Wait for the signal to occur.

There are two Wall Street adages:

1. "The majority is usually wrong."

2. "If it is obvious, it is obviously wrong."

Chapter 14 – Conclusion

A few simple rules

1. Conserve capital at all costs. Never place more than 10% in any one trade.

2. Never act solely on advice.

3. Ignore impending dividends. Never hold or buy solely to collect a coming dividend.

4. CUT LOSSES. This is the most important rule. Adhere to stop-losses rigidly. Charting is a mechanical practice, there is no room for emotions or gut feelings. It will be impossible to get it right every time.

5. Let profits run. Wait for trends to be clearly broken. The trend is your friend.

True understanding comes through explanation. Put yourself to this test. Sit down with someone who has a mutual interest. This could be a friend, at an investment club, a letter or fax to your broker, or a presentation to your other half. Show them graphs of your shares and ones you are about to buy. If you have software to help you do this on screen, all the better. Now explain your actions as simply as possible. Then try to get this person to give you a brief summary of this explanation.

CHAPTER TWO

The Graph Itself

● ●

'Never forecast with a ruler. Nothing moves in a straight line.' This is a good principle in business and equally good in markets. Trend lines are great, but always recognise that future price movement will be different from any line you choose to draw.

Before we dive head first into understanding trends, it is worth taking a glance at a few price histories chosen at random to try to build a picture for what is going on. Having said that the graph is 90% of the story, it occurs to me we had better take a good look at why. This should also help investors to understand the approach to take in moving on with deeper analysis. You need to get to a point where you like a graph because you can see what is happening or you don't, because you can't, at a glance.

I spend a great deal of time looking at graphs with Updata staff and clients, brokers and experienced technical analysts. This process is not dissimilar to going to an art gallery with a friend. Each person will have favourite pictures and then there is an excitement of a consensus when you find something you both like. Technical analysis is more art than science. The more you watch graphs, the more you get a feel for different types of behaviour and patterns in price movement. Sometimes it is difficult to put the understanding you build into words. You start to see things you never noticed. You can even begin to feel you have discovered a new technique. Don't get too carried away. We get approached at Updata almost as regularly as once a week with the latest earth shattering discovery. Most of all if you find something that works for you consistently, and I recommend you test it heavily before committing money to it, keep at it. Everyone will begin to find his own favourite forms of analysis, but most will be returned to first principles for the bigger picture.

It was suggested,in the conclusion of *Profit from your PC*, that the explanation of a subject built true understanding. I am always encouraged when I see a couple of people at our user group evenings sharing ideas about a graph. If you have a friend down the road or an interested family member, why not ask him to sit down and look at some graphs with you. I find it refreshingly fun to take this light hearted approach occasionally.

So here we produce some graphs with some commentary, which is merely stating what to many will be the obvious. Again I have stuck to shares in top UK companies, as the graphs tend to be more interesting with high trading volume behind the shares. I have done this simply by taking the FT-SE 100 shares and scrolled through each graph one by one and pulling out a few that seem interesting at a glance.

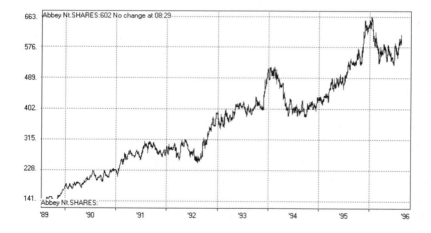

Source: Updata

This share has been a strong performer over the years although they have not performed well in even years. Sideways in 1992 though a strong recovery towards the end, a fall of 20% in 1994 and a similar fall in 1996. The share has not fallen below support, and these corrections aside, has always maintained a strong upward trend.

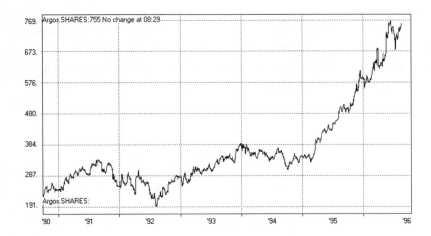

Source: Updata

This share traded virtually sideways for the first half of the nineties with a strong breakout in early 1995. In eighteen months it has more than doubled. This is very tight trading, not the longer bigger swings in price of the preceding years. There is an increased level of volatility in more recent months with price behaviour becoming more erratic.

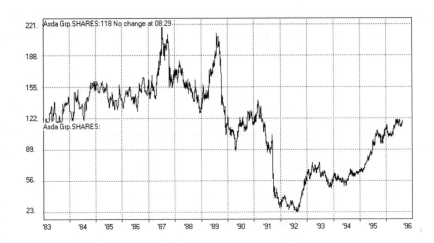

Source: Updata

The chart at the bottom of page 43 shows that after a fall from grace in the late eighties and early nineties, this has become a clear case of recovery. While the share price is building a more predictable trading pattern over the past few months, it seems to be having some difficulty getting above the 120p mark. There are not many top UK companies that have shown a four fold performance over the past four years and still at around half their all time high.

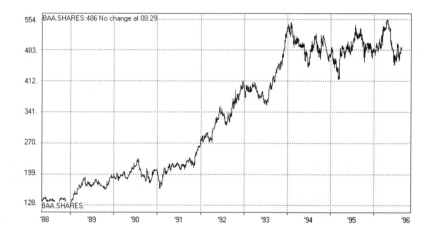

Source: Updata

This share performed very strongly for several years and has gone sideways, with a much wider trading range, for the last few. It can't trade sideways forever, will it move up or down. One to watch for a move in either direction.

> "The graph gives you 90% of the picture.
>
> Understanding the trends gives a further 9%.
>
> Other forms of technical analysis give you the rest and often serve as confirmation."

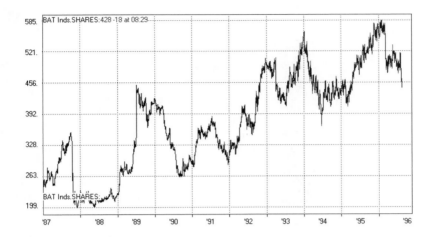

Source: Updata

A share in a sector that has fallen out of favour. The share has traded very erratically as a result. Despite these factors, this stock has not fallen below critical support levels, though it seems to be really testing long term support now. This stock is very capable of dramatic moves in either direction.

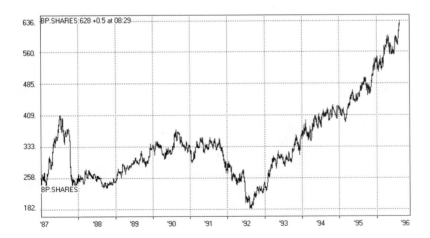

Source: Updata

After a fairly lacklustre performance over several years, this share has behaved beautifully. Looking back over the history, crash of 1987 apart, the stock has always behaved in tight trading ranges.

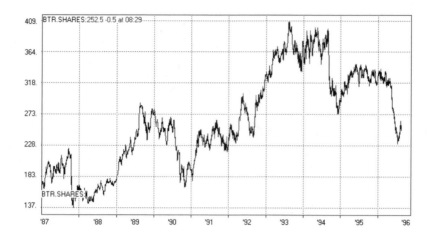

Source: Updata

This stock is the inverse of a recovery. It demonstrates how downward trending stocks can often have sharp movements down, with weak attempts at recovery. The distance between these troughs in the downtrend seems to be about a year and a half. Where will it be in eighteen months' time?

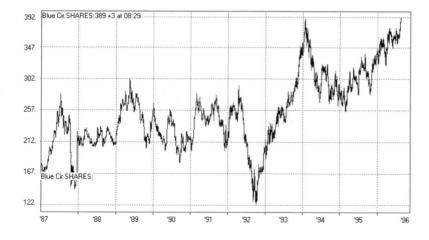

Source: Updata

A stock that traded sideways, then uncharacteristically broke down, followed by a dramatic recovery. Blue Circle looks set to break into new ground. If it does, it could rally strongly.

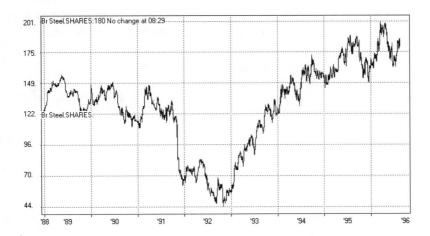

Source: Updata

After a breakout of the sideways movement, this share found the bottom twice and then recovered. The uptrend has been slowing and widening over the past couple of years. Will it roll over into a downtrend or go for a second rally?

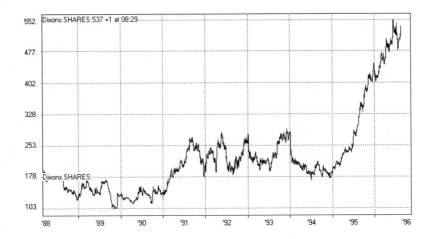

Source: Updata

After a long period of sideways movement, this graph shows 'hockey stick' like performance. It is inevitable that this steepness of trend cannot be maintained and we are starting to see some volatility and a rolling over.

With graphing software one can go on for ages doing this by scrolling graphs one after the other on screen. Graphs that do attract interest entice one to place some analysis, mainly trend lines, on the graphs to illustrate the points further.

CHAPTER THREE

Trends

● ●

'The trend is your friend' is probably the most important adage for the investor using graphs for making investment decisions. You need to establish trends before carrying out any further 'analysis. If you cannot spot a trend then it is really questionable whether further technical analysis will be useful. The exception may be a clear identification of a cycle period and the use of a periodic indicator. Clear cyclical behaviour is much harder to find, with examples being considerably less numerous than graphs following trends.

Trend analysis can really be broken down into two main types, 1) trend channel analysis (auto-trends for Updata software users), and 2) individual trend lines.

Trend channels are best for graphs where you can almost see the trend channel. This is also ideally suited to using a PC. The trend channel is a calculated central regression line shifted two standard deviations above and below this central line. For selecting the data being sampled, one needs to choose what appears to be the beginning and end of the trend. The beginning is normally marked by a trough or a change in direction, the end by a peak.

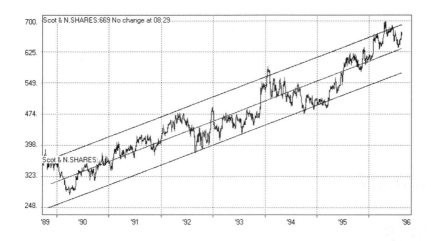

Source: Updata

The graph above shows the central regression line, or central trend, about which the price movement oscillates. The channel is defined by the outer boundaries. This is very useful for building a quick understanding of where the price lies within the general trend.

Normal Price Behaviour within a Trend Channel

If you look at behaviour within trend channels for long enough, you notice that there is a common format for price movement. I have no knowledge of this being documented, but it is a characteristic that appears to be true more often than not. These two diagrams are very simplistic, but should illustrate the general point – that dramatic movement within the trend normally occurs in the direction of the trend.

Uptrends

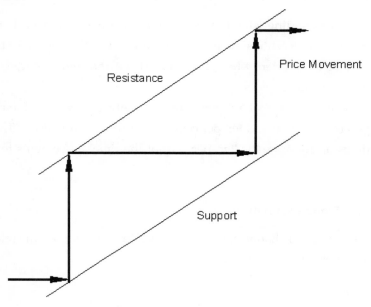

Downtrends

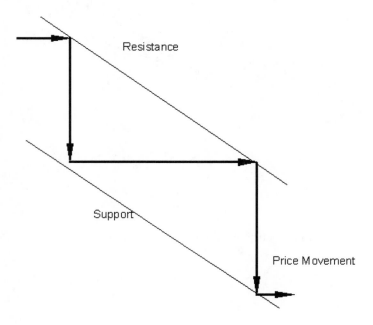

Timing in the Trend Channel

The advantage of understanding what is happening in the trend channel is that you can time your buy and sell decisions, such that you don't sell at the bottom or buy at the top. People are often amazed when it is pointed out that most shares spend most of their time going sideways.

Hence the point earlier that markets spend ninety per cent of their time thinking about where to go next and ten per cent of their time getting there. The key is to use these times of the dramatic 'ten per cent of the time' movements to your advantage.

Some examples of Trend channels

To illustrate how to use trend channels, I have placed trend channels on the relevant bits of each of the graphs used earlier.

Source: Updata

This graph shows the main uptrend and the trends within it.

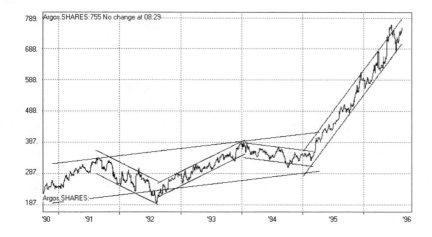

Source: Updata

Four trends or two? Notice the sharp moves upwards in the narrower uptrend.

Source: Updata

This sideways movement in share price may be part of a bigger picture, ie. a move across the uptrend. A move upwards out of this sideways channel would normally be considered to be a breakout, though looking at it as part of the longer term it may be simply a move to the top of the trading range. This is useful, as it gives a feel for the likely extent of the breakout.

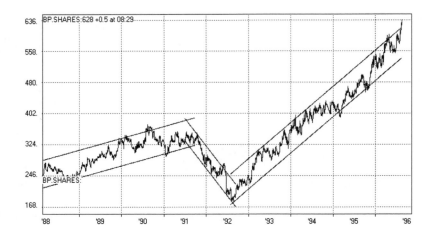

Source: Updata

Whether going up or down, this is a very well behaved stock. It moves in tight trend channels, making the beginning and end of each trend easier to call. Are we seeing some early signs of unpredictability at the end of the trend?

Source: Updata

Here in BTR the moves down within the downtrend are very dramatic.

Source: Updata

The Bass graph has changed in character with the breakout from predominantly sideways movement.

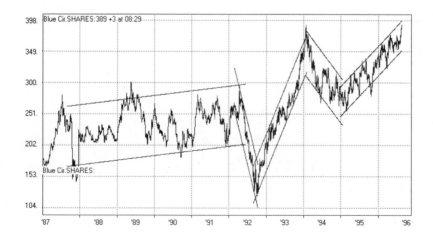

Source: Updata

From sideways movement to tight trends in either direction. These tight new trends could be forming the basis of a longer term wider uptrend.

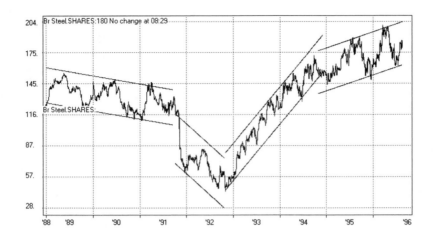

Source: Updata

A not so steep downtrend, then a steeper one, followed by a steep uptrend and then a not so steep one. What next?

Source: Updata

Breakouts don't come bigger than this. Last time the rise was followed by a long sideways move. What this time?

Using Trend Lines

Trend lines are more precise, but take more time and skill to place on graphs. Trend channels almost do the artistic interpretation for you. With trend lines you are left to do it yourself.

Support and resistance

Trend lines can be classified as either support or resistance. Support is a trend line below the share price movement and, as the name implies, this is normally a threshold that is difficult to cross. Similarly, resistance is an upper limit which normally restricts price movement.

To illustrate lines of support and resistance, the same examples are used with the trend lines drawn on manually (Updata users – drag and drop lines). The key to placing trend lines on a graph is to draw lines of support across the troughs and lines of resistance joining the peaks. Ideally you need three or more points for a valid trend line. Often the points don't join up perfectly, so it is necessary to judge a best fit. Sometimes intra-day high and low values, or spikes, will be very important for drawing the trend line. Other times these spikes will need to be ignored in order to get points to join up. There is no fixed rule on this, but you need to ask yourself, is this the best fit?

Many technical analysts argue that trend lines must take account of all price movements. The problem with this is that perfect examples are very few and far between, thus increasing the workload in using analysis and decreasing useful deductions that may be made. Don't be too rigid.

Those who have studied navigation will appreciate that a small discrepancy in course bearing on starting a journey can have a significant impact on reaching the destination. One degree will protract through to one mile out after sixty miles. Much the same is true of trend lines. The consequence may be that the trend line is significantly, out giving signals either when it is too early (ie. not signals) or when it is too late. Therefore if you are forced to make variance on a spike, make it on the earlier part of the graph. These points will be less significant than the last peak. It is easy to mess around with a ruler on a printed graph before arriving at the line. Those using trend lines with a mouse may find they need a few attempts at getting the line right.

Some investors who have taken up charting techniques have vented their frustration when they can't get their trend lines precise. You can't be too much of a perfectionist. A little flexibility often comes in useful. To some this may not seem terribly relevant, but for those who do have difficulty, give the above analogy some consideration next time you have a dilemma with the kind of situation on page 58.

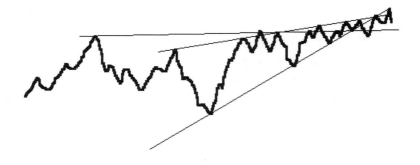

Which trend line?

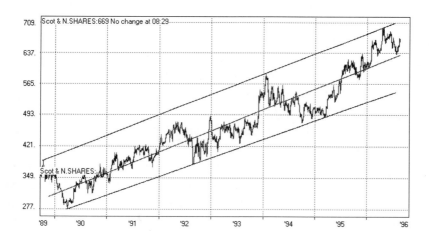

Source: Updata

Here you can see that drawing the trend lines manually has much the same result as using a trend channel. This is due to the fact that this share behaves very well within these boundaries. This also makes its behaviour much more predictable than most.

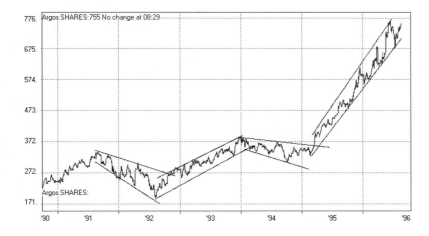

Source: Updata

The current support line is very clear cut, the share price has touched this line several times, giving a strong confirmation of support. It is worth looking at the differences with the trend channel covered earlier in the chapter.

Source: Updata

Support sometimes becomes resistance, as it did here at one point in early 1991 and a few times in 1992.

Source: Updata

Is this share trading sideways and pausing for breath, or has it fallen through support and out of its uptrend? A fall through 417p would mark a move out of the sideways trading range.

Source: Updata

Only a manually drawn long term support line can give a clear indication of whether support has been breached or not.

Source: Updata

Manually drawn trend lines give a much clearer indication of a recovery (1992) or a breakout (late 1993)

Source: Updata

There are few stocks where the picture has changed so much over the years. Can it fall further? Don't be fooled into thinking it can't.

Source: Updata

It is currently difficult to find the upper limit on this stock. Could we have spotted that it was breaking new ground in late 1993 or early 1995?

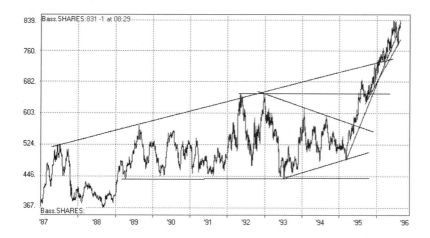

Source: Updata

Is Bass faltering? One trend line says yes, another says no. Could we have spotted this spectacular breakout in early 1995?

Source: Updata

A few pence below its all time high, can it break into new ground, or will it reverse as violently as it did in 1994?

Source: Updata

Steep trends cannot be maintained forever, price movement often breaks down to a less steep line, and again.

Source: Updata

After years of sideways movement, Dixons had some catching up to do – fast. Where next?

Trend lines or channels

Having used both methods in these examples, channels are ideal for quick or initial assessment. They work especially well for tight trending stocks and often provide a good first view of the trend. Trend lines give an additional level of understanding with more clear indication of levels of support and resistance. Therefore each of these methods is valid and they become more powerful when used together.

Breakdown or Correction

Corrections are healthy, but breakdowns can seriously damage your wealth. Once you are invested in a trending stock, you should be happy to see regular corrections within the trend channel. A kind of two steps forward one step back movement. This is encouraging, as it is one of the key characteristics for predictable stock price movement.

The key difference with a breakdown, the reverse of a breakout, is a fall through a key line of support.

High Risk, High Return –
the double whammy near the trend line

Share price movement in a trend channel can be a bit like flying an aeroplane, the exciting bits are take-off and landing. In an uptrend the nerve-racking time is on or near support, where a sell signal may be given. In a downtrend, the opportunity to buy may arise if resistance is clearly breached.

The risk in an uptrend is that as the share price approaches the line of support, it should bounce up and head for the top of the trend channel, but could carry on through support wandering into the larger unsafe zone, shown below.

Uptrends

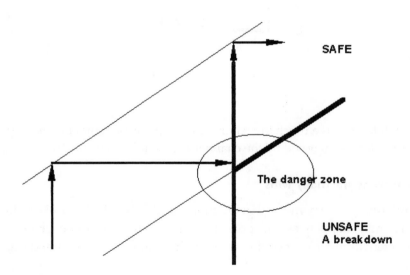

So, what do you do as this begins to happen? The key point is not to be too eager, anticipating, to sell before a breach actually occurs. A couple more tips are given overleaf, but if in doubt use a stop-loss, covered later.

Downtrends

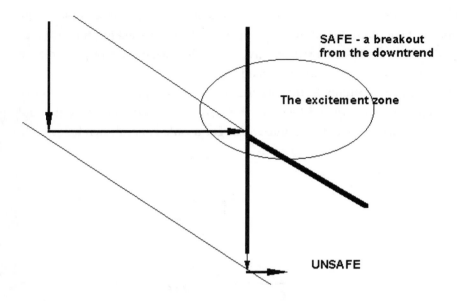

SAFE - a breakout
from the downtrend

The excitement zone

UNSAFE

In a downtrend, while there is a much bigger area for the price movement to recover, the move will normally be governed by the channel and hence will be down.

The longer term trend normally wins

This is a helpful tip, but remember that in time all trends will be broken. In considering what may happen as the price line approaches the trend channel boundary, it is often useful to ascertain whether there are any other trends or patterns present.

CHAPTER FOUR

Pattern Recognition

● ●

A number of readers of *Profit from your PC* and Updata users have asked for assistance in understanding patterns. At Updata we have spent a number of years researching the idea of software recognising patterns in share price histories. We are now seeing processing power of personal computers reaching the point where the massive amount of data sampling required is possible. A bigger issue is developing the software algorithms to interpret patterns with the right level of artistic licence. There are still some things which the human eye can interpret at a glance that PCs find very difficult. Try writing the algorithm for peak detection and you will see what I mean. It becomes dependent upon definitions, when is a peak a peak and when is it not. Then the definitions come into question.

In this chapter we look at some common price patterns that have received a high level of acclaim over the years. Be careful not to start jumping in and feeling the need to attribute a pattern. They often don't exist. I frequently meet investors who have taken the study of charting further and then feel the need to identify what is happening within a few seconds. For instance, 'Oh, that's obviously a reverse head and shoulders'. Please remember these movements are often part of a bigger, or longer term, picture.

Triangles

There are five main types of triangle pattern shown below:

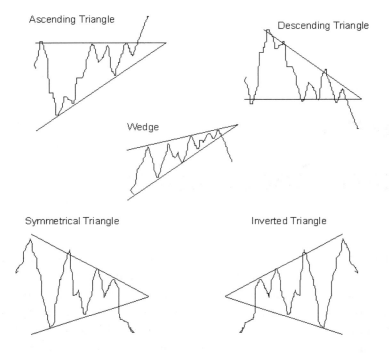

A few rules with triangles:

1. There must be at least two reversal points on each trend line for a triangle formation to exist.

2. The longer side of the triangle normally wins out, as the longer term trend line is more powerful.

3. The breakout will invariably occur in the direction that the triangle is pointing except for a wedge (ie. ascending triangle indicates a breakout upwards, descending downwards).

4. If the triangle points in a sideways direction, or very close to it, the breakout will occur in either direction and is often very dramatic (ie. symmetrical triangle).

5. The breakout should occur around two thirds of the way along the triangle, except in the cases of the inverted and the wedge.

6. The larger the triangle (length of time over which it has formed), the bigger the breakout.

7. The inverted triangle (sometimes called a fan) is not very reliable.

8. A wedge pattern (where both lines slope in the same direction) normally marks an imminent reversal or breakout in the opposite direction.

One should not go out of one's way to remember all of these points, but it is well worth becoming practised at spotting these formations. A few real life examples follow shortly.

Flags and Pennants

The patterns below can be more difficult to identify and often form part of the bigger picture within a trend channel. For instance a dramatic move up, followed by a period of sideways movement. These can also be inverted for downtrends. It is worth remembering that a stock which has fallen dramatically and is now trading sideways may not have hit its floor and might actually be pausing for breath before another big fall.

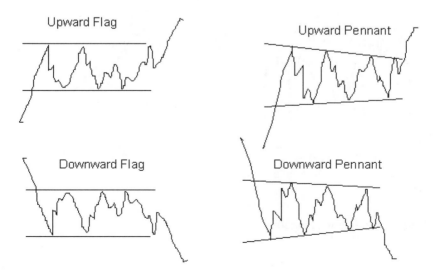

Upward Flag

Upward Pennant

Downward Flag

Downward Pennant

Source: Updata

An ascending triangle with BA.

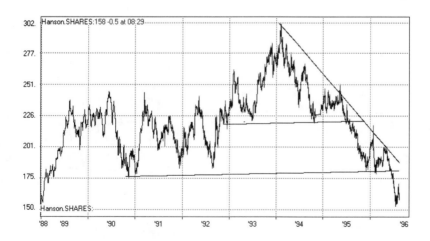

Source: Updata

Descending triangles with Hanson.

Source: Updata

A symmetrical triangle with BAT.

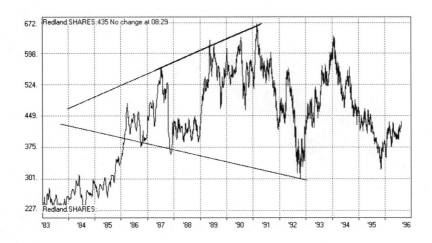

Source: Updata

The problem with an inverted triangle is it leaves a much broader scope for price movement than the narrowing price squeeze of the other types of triangle.

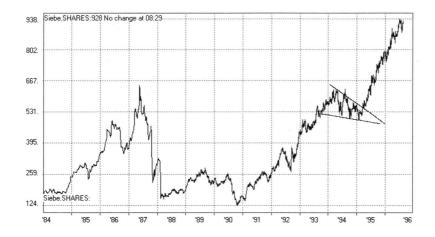

Source: Updata

Wedges can be very powerful, but also difficult to find and identify.

Source: Updata

There is not a lot of difference between flags and pennants. These patterns are often attributed to triangles incorrectly, as the breakout is occurring well before two thirds of the way along what is actually an acute triangle. Ascending and descending triangles are normally more shaped like an equilateral triangle.

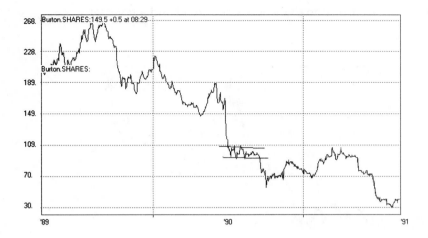

Source: Updata

The downside equivalent for a flag.

Fans

Fan patterns, below, arise due to the natural inability of steep trends to be maintained. Normally when these patterns occur, the third fan line being broken signals a full reversal. This third line, however, can often be the longer term trend which serves as a strong support level. This principle can be employed with uptrends or downtrends and serves as a useful background to understanding reversals and corrections.

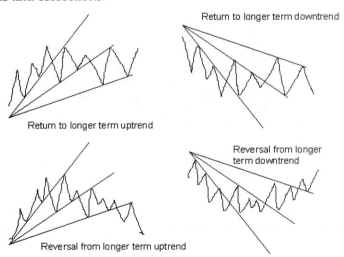

Return to longer term downtrend

Return to longer term uptrend

Reversal from longer term uptrend

Reversal from longer term downtrend

73

Some real life examples of each type of fan are given below. There is a critical difference between a correction to the less steep trend and a reversal.

Source: Updata

The big test. Can this long term support level be maintained?

Source: Updata

A long awaited reversal still hasn't materialised.

Source: Updata

At first glance Inchcape seem to be turning the corner, but a look at the longer term shows a fall through long term support. Not a recovery yet, more a full reversal.

Source: Updata

An upside reversal at last.

Rolling Over and Topping Out and the reverse

Before moving on to some other patterns, let's look at the more general concept of shares that gradually run out of steam. Deceleration may occur via a number of the patterns outlined in this chapter. Whether you attribute a fan or double top pattern you may just be happy to understand that the price movement is undergoing a gradual change in direction. The two examples below are sweeping curves illustrating 'rolling over, topping out' patterns and 'rolling under, bottoming out' patterns respectively. These patterns almost look like curved trend channels.

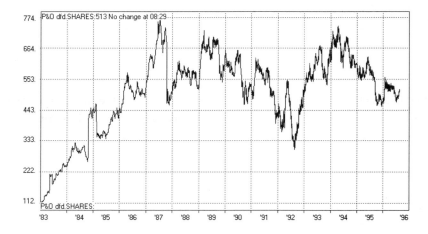

Source: Updata

At first glance the behaviour is a little erratic, but this share has rolled over twice in the past decade.

> "Short term price movements are
> often part of a bigger,
> longer term, picture."

Source: Updata

There are few examples of a bottoming out, long term reversal that come close to this one.

Tops and Bottoms

Some quite simple patterns that can often be spotted during reversals are double tops and bottoms or triple tops and bottoms.

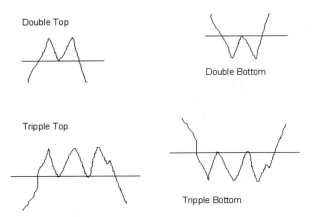

Double Top

Double Bottom

Tripple Top

Tripple Bottom

One real life example of each of these appears below.

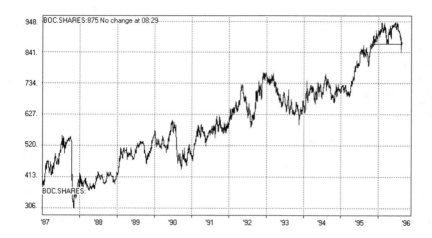

Source: Updata

BOC look as if they have just formed a double top.

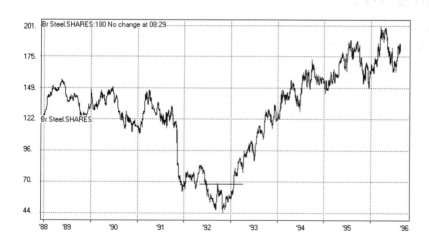

Source: Updata

A double bottom in the early nineties.

Source: Updata

A possible triple top.

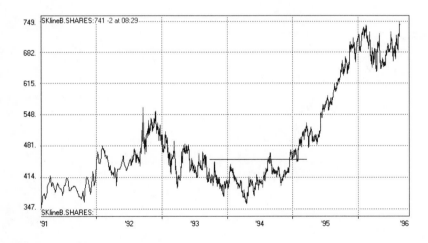

Source: Updata

Clear cases of triple bottoms are harder to find, but some would argue this is one.

I find that tops and bottoms tend to show up better on intra-day charts or those zoomed in that show the daily high/lows as spikes. A couple of examples are given overleaf. Some Updata users swear by these spikes and refer to them as 'rabbit's teeth'.

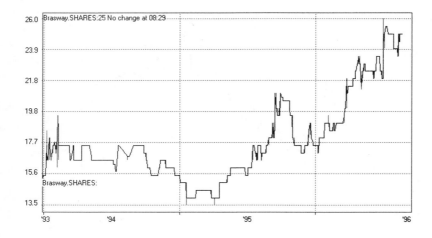

Source: Updata

These spikes were wide apart in early 1995, but they showed that the market was happy to pick up the shares at this low price, twice.

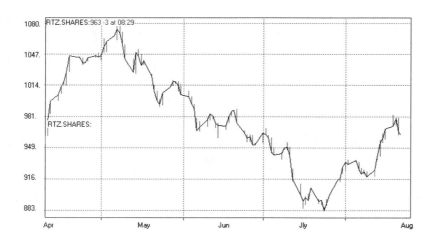

Source: Updata

Double spikes at the top in May and double spikes near the bottom in July.

Head and Shoulders

One of the best known patterns used by technical analysts is the head and shoulders. Many people claim they work every time. I still find them quite difficult to find and that they seem to work only some of the time.

Anyway, this is what they look like.

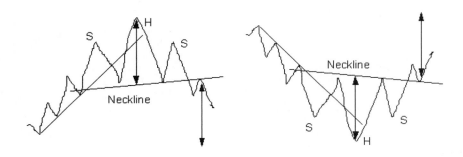

Source: Updata

There are a number of key requirements for a head and shoulders pattern:

1. A prior uptrend.

2. A left shoulder on heavy volume followed by a corrective dip.

3. A rally into new highs, but on lighter volume.

4. A decline that moves below the level of the peak of the previous shoulder and approaches the previous trough, forming the neckline.

5. A third rally on noticeably light volume that fails to reach the level of peak of the head.

6. A close below the neckline.

7. A return move back to the neckline followed by new lows (confirmation).

The resulting decline is said to be the height of the head to the neckline. The reverse or inverted head and shoulders works in the opposite manner. The neckline can slope upwards or downwards to some extent for the pattern to work. A few real examples follow:

Source: Updata

Many claim the stockmarket crash of 1987 was a head and shoulders. The FT-SE 100 pattern was weak, as there was no conformation. The Dow Jones index which led the fall did have a point of conformation though the left shoulder was very weak.

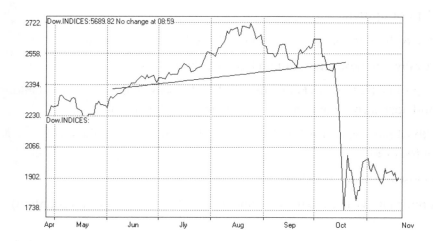

Source: Updata

Source: Updata

Head and Shoulders requires a good degree of artistic interpretation. The head may often have a number of peaks. It is difficult to find price movement that follows the conceptual diagrams outlined before.

Source: Updata

Which neckline?

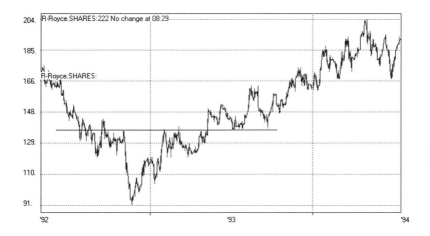

Source: Updata

The reverse head and shoulders.

Confirmation

One of the most important factors that I have noticed while watching markets over the years (though I have not seen it clearly documented) is that of 'confirmation'. When trend lines are breached, especially in the pattern formations outlined in this chapter, a return to the trend from the other side, to confirm it, is potentially very powerful. I have derived this from head and shoulders and also notice it frequently with triangles, pennants, fans and even support becoming resistance.

The most potent aspect of this type of move in price is shortly after a breakout and it is often well worth waiting for confirmation. The upside of this is you avoid buying into a failed breakout. The downside is you may miss the beginning of the run. The same principle can be applied to breakdowns, but it appears to be a much more common characteristic for the move up. It is important to understand that confirmation doesn't occur on the trend line, but when the previous peak in the new territory is passed.

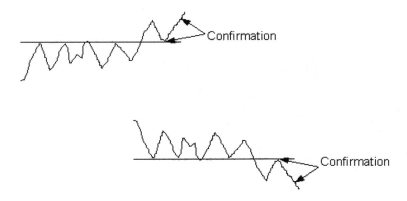

Source: Updata

A few real life examples are given below:

Source: Updata

Confirmation can often happen very quickly, even just intra-day.

Source: Updata

At other times the price seems to dither back and forth before running.

Source: Updata

Even very long term lines can be tested for confirmation. Who would believe this share could really fall further!

CHAPTER FIVE

Comparative Analysis

● ●

PCs are brilliant for overlaying graphs for comparison. There are two main types of comparative analysis:

1. Comparing a graph against the market

2. Comparing a graph against comparable companies

and there are two main types of overlay graph

1. Rebased Overlays

2. Relative Overlays

A rebased overlay takes the overlay graph and adjusts every price such that the starting points of the graphs are the same, allowing you to see both graphs on the same axis. A relative overlay effectively divides one graph by the other, such that each data point is divided by the corresponding data point on the overlay, and then rebases it to fit on the same axis. Rebased overlays are useful for identifying convergence and divergence from the market. They are also helpful in comparative analysis with a number of related companies. Relative overlays are great for understanding true performance in relation to the market.

Overlays are probably best illustrated here by the following examples of graphs.

Market Comparison

Source: Updata

British Aerospace, the lower graph, at first glance looks like it has run well ahead of the market. An FT-SE 100 index rebased overlay shows it has been playing catch-up.

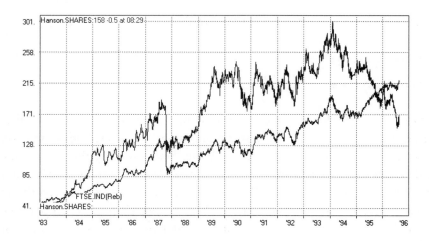

Source: Updata

Years of out-performance come to an end as Hanson crosses down through FT-SE 100 index.

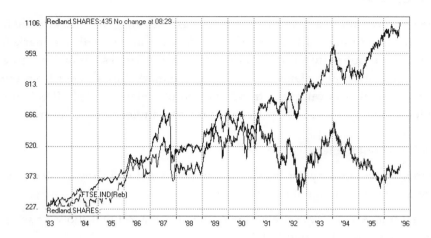

Source: Updata

Some graphs show a massive divergence from the market.

Company Comparison

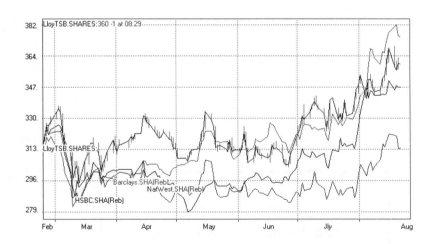

Source: Updata

Banks over the last six months at a glance. This kind of analysis, clearer with a colour monitor on a PC, helps show quickly which stock is under-performing. If you are getting strong buy signals based on trend analysis, it can be useful to determine if there is any upside with overlays.

Market Relatives

Fund managers normally use market relatives, as they like to measure their performance relative to the market. Anyone can perform in line with the market, the real test is to out-perform the market. Market relatives show the true performance of the share at a glance by removing the market movement from the share price movement. You can place trend lines on the relative graph. Breakouts and recoveries on the relative can be extremely powerful indicators to a reversal.

Some key points about the relative are:

1. A share that trades sideways or rises less than the market will show a fall on the market relative, even though it may be rising.

2. A share that trades sideways or falls slower than the market will show a rise on the relative, even though it may be falling.

3. The market relative normally oscillates gently over the long term.

4. A flat market relative means the share follows the market very closely.

5. Market relative graphs are not useful for shares that are not typical of the market, such as small unusual companies.

6. The same points can be drawn from doing comparable company relatives.

> "Anyone can perform in line
> with the market. The real test
> is to out-perform it."

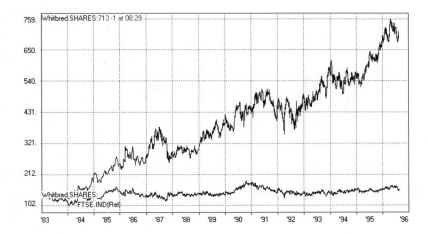

Source: Updata

The relative in this case also helps to identify Whitbread's long term cycle against the market.

Source: Updata

The relative clearly showed long term under-performance and helped identify changes in direction. The breakout signal occurred a few months earlier on the relative than on the actual graph. This breakout was also significant, as it was the first time in several years that Pilkington started to out-perform the market.

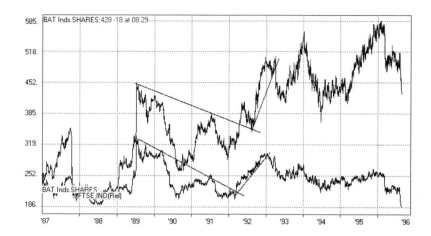

Source: Updata

Market Relatives don't come more erratic than this. Historically the relative gave earlier signals, except for the sharp moves recently.

Comparable Company Relatives

Source: Updata

Commercial Union relative to Royal Sun Alliance

CHAPTER SIX

Cyclical Behaviour

● ●

In *Profit from your PC* we touched on the concept of identifying cyclical shares and their cycle periods. There have been a number of requests to enlarge on this. It seems that investors are quite excited about identifying cycles on the basis that it will help them predict where a share price will be in a given number of days or weeks. This can be dangerous because, like trends, cycles can be broken at any time.

Identifying cycles, wherever possible, is not only useful in itself but is vital for selecting the appropriate period for indicators that require an averaging period to be selected.

The key characteristics of a cycle are:

1. A repetitive wave form or retracement

2. A central axis – about which the oscillation occurs

3. A cycle period length

4. An amplitude – the height of the wave from the central axis

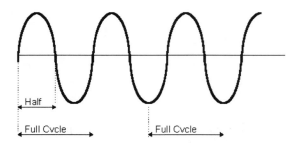

Taking this simplified form and relating it to more erratic share movements can be difficult at the best of times and impossible at the worst.

One of the first things to consider is that the central axis will normally be sloping, skewing the overall picture to appear something like the diagrams below.

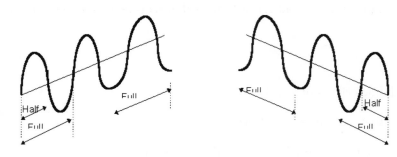

I have tried to find a number of shares where it is fairly easy to identify cycles. This is harder than spotting trends. The central regression line, already discussed under

Trends in Chapter 3, is helpful in verifying cycles. A software ruler function also helps me measure the number of days between two points on the cycle. I use the sideways arrows, to highlight an estimated cycle length. These are drawn from any one of the following three: 1) peak to peak, 2) trough to trough, 3) start to start (crossing up through central axis).

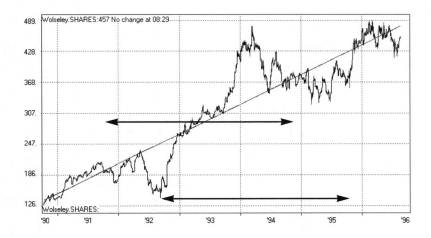

Source: Updata

The length of the lines shown on this picture respectively are: 3yrs 2days, and 2yrs 280days. These longer term cycles are not much use for indicators.

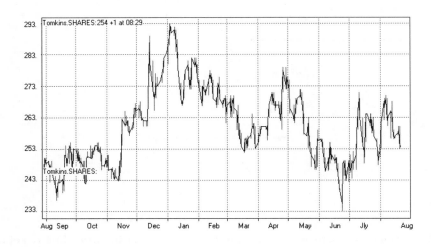

Source: Updata

Using another approach in the chart on page 95, we look back over one year to establish the shorter term periods. As a quick guide we can see there are normally two peaks and two troughs in any one month. One complete cycle consists of one peak and one trough, which implies a short term cycle period of 15 days. Taking this further we can also see three peaks and three troughs in the year implying a longer term (probably medium term) cycle of 120 days.

Source: Updata

Looking at Tesco over the past year, it seems to have a cycle of around three months.

Source: Updata

TI Group is less clear. On screen you can run your finger over the price line to get a feel. On paper with a pen may be even clearer.

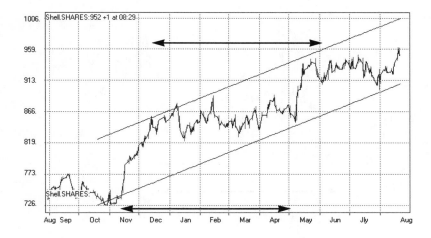

Source: Updata

A trend channel can often help to spot cycles.

I always find that this process is a bit long and tedious which is why I favour trends. For those that do use indicators that utilise periods, such as moving averages, it is very important to use an averaging period as close to the cycle period as possible. Otherwise you are either sampling bits of the cycle more than once or not the whole cycle.

Moving averages can be a very useful tool for removing the distraction of the day to day fluctuations when looking at share price histories. If you have difficulty spotting the cycle period, an average can often make things clearer.

> **"Remember – make the**
>
> **trend your friend."**

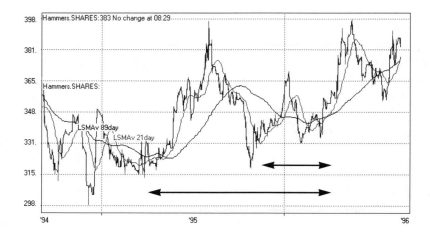

Source: Updata

Here the moving averages help spot shorter and longer term cycles by smoothing the daily fluctuations.

Fibonacci, a twelfth century mathematician, developed a number series from his study of natural cycles –

1, 2, (2+1) 3,

(3+2) 5, (5+3) 8, (8+5) 13,

(13+8) 21, (21+13) 34, (34+21) 55,

(55+34) 89, (89+55) 144. . .

Each number adds the previous two numbers. These numbers were used by the famous Wall Street trader W.D. Gann with tremendous success and have since been shown to work with a fairly high degree of accuracy over time. I find using these numbers to find the moving average period that has given the best signals historically is the easiest form of cycle based analysis. A few examples follow:

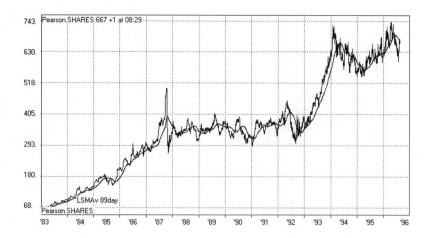

Source: Updata

The 89 day average worked fairly well for Pearson up until 1994. The bigger swings in price means that it is no longer effective as a longer term indicator. It is often useful to look a long way back to see how well a particular average has worked.

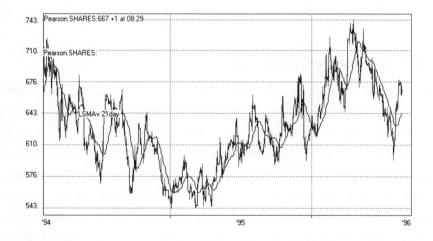

Source: Updata

The 21 day moving average seems to be working for spotting short term reversals.

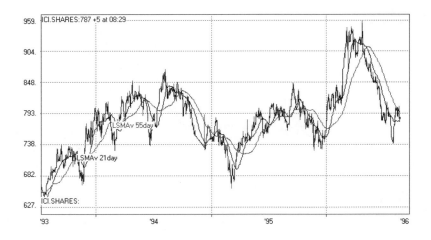

Source: Updata

Here you can see that the 21 day moving average was crossed more frequently than the 55 day.

Sensitivity versus Early Signals

One of the problems with moving averages is that they are lagging indicators, meaning they often give late signals. If you get them giving earlier signals they become too sensitive, ie. giving false signals. I find the longer term ones tend to work better due to the fact that shorter term trends or cycles are more easily broken. One way to address this is to use a weighted moving average. This assigns proportionally more priority to the more recent points in calculating the average. This effectively skews the average line in such a way as not to make it more sensitive, but to pull the signals earlier as on page 101. The 55 day weighted average worked much better on ICI shares recently.

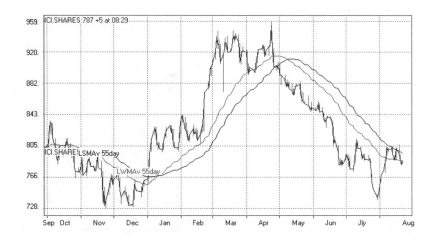

Source: Updata

Moving averages used in conjunction with one another

Using two moving averages together can give useful buy and sell signals. One of the problems of using one moving average is that the price line can cross it briefly a number of times, giving false signals. A second shorter term average will smooth these fluctuations such that the averages cross each other to give clearer signals. These signals are known as crosses and they are shown on page 102.

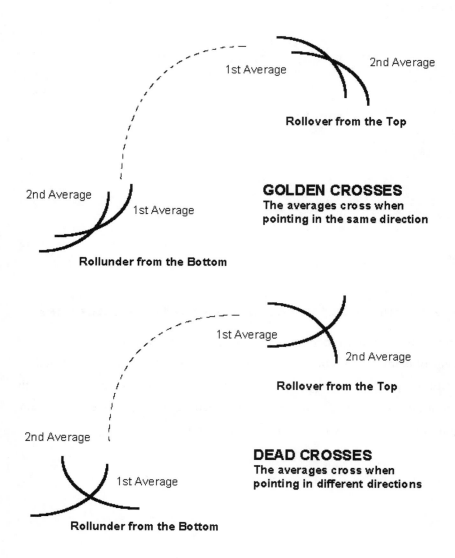

Rollover from the Top

2nd Average

1st Average

Rollunder from the Bottom

GOLDEN CROSSES
**The averages cross when
pointing in the same direction**

Rollover from the Top

DEAD CROSSES
**The averages cross when
pointing in different directions**

Rollunder from the Bottom

As their names imply Golden Crosses and Dead Crosses give good and poor signals respectively. The key point to remember is that the averages should be pointing in the same direction when they cross.

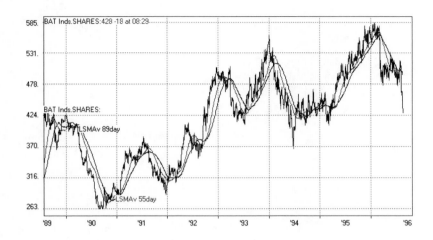

Source: Updata

The golden crosses gave the best signals for BAT. The dead crosses didn't.

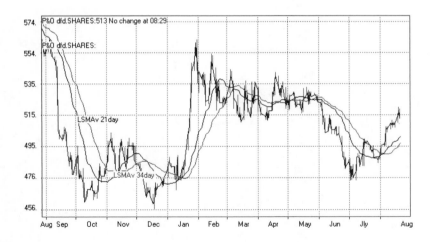

Source: Updata

The dead crosses occurred where the averages were running flat and weaving across one another in the spring of 1996.

CHAPTER SEVEN

Stop-losses

● ●

I was told many years ago, when speculating in the property market, **'Always leave ten per cent for the other guy.' This is one of the most valuable lessons in investment.**

The diagram on page 106 shows that you should probably leave twenty per cent for the other guys – ten per cent at each end. It is these first and last ten per cents that are by far the most risky bit of an investment, as it is where the market uncertainty reigns.

You will also remember that the market spends 90% of its time thinking about where to move and 10% of its time doing it. This 10% of time is the most profitable time and the annual rate of return is increased due to the shorter period over which profit is achieved. The first and last 10% of the price movement, the reversal period, can account for most of the time.

And we all know, time is money, though some investors seem to be particularly adept at forgetting this by tucking their poor performing shares away.

The rest of this chapter is dedicated to explaining the stop-loss system to you.

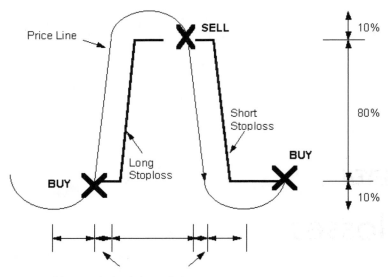

Short periods of dramatic movement

Using this principle means you wait to see the turnaround from dramatic moves in price. It helps you avoid buying into a failed recovery or moving too soon into one. On the selling side, the downside is that you do sit out the reversal. However, the upside is that there is more certainty of a finished rally in the price.

So many investors buy things because they have a gut feeling that a price is cheap and can't fall further, or sell because they think it is expensive and can't believe it can go any higher. Worse than this, many investors don't buy when something has moved up ten per cent from a low because they feel that it has run too far and they have missed the boat.

Even worse still, the greatest sin in investment, many investors don't sell when a price has fallen back 10% from the high because they feel they have missed a better opportunity to get out and would like a second chance at the highest price. **Leave the ten per cent before the reversal to someone else and wait for the ten per cent after the reversal to deal.**

Taking this principle a step further you can increase overall profits by trying to spend only this segment of time in the various stocks you trade. This should lead to a compounding effect shown opposite.

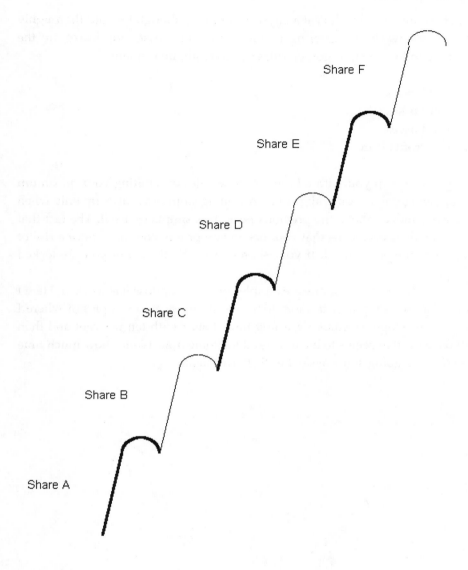

Share F

Share E

Share D

Share C

Share B

Share A

Of course this is much more easily said than done, but setting this as your goal should be part of your strategy. The less time you spend in stocks that are falling or going sideways, the more chance you have approaching this optimised state. In reality you will have a number of different shares in various states at any one time. Make sure their individual stock positions lie somewhere on these walking stick shaped curves.

Using Stop-losses

If you have trouble using technical analysis techniques, though I would thoroughly recommend you work at mastering trends at the very least, stop-losses are the easiest way to follow the four golden rules of successful investment.

1. **Cut Losses**
2. **Cut Losses**
3. **Cut Losses**
4. **Let Profits Run**

Stop-losses help you with all four of these rules by limiting your maximum loss and allowing you to run with profits. A trailing stop-loss moves up only when the share price moves above the previous peak. It is simplicity itself. The fact that the stop-loss moves up means that you lock in any profits you make once a rise of the stop-loss value is achieved. If your shares rise 10%, thereafter you are locked into pure profit.

It is easy to produce countless examples of how stop-loss has worked. Here I have chosen a few. Graphs with more than one stop-loss are examples of where I have not got the stop-loss value right first time. I start with ten per cent and then adjust it to a level that seems to have worked for some time. Notice how much time stop-losses spend going sideways – the 90/10 rule again.

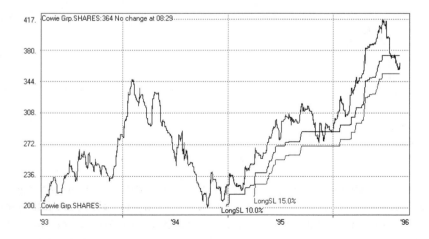

Source: Updata

Cowie Group seems to be better with a 15% stop-loss, 10% would have taken you out twice on this healthy rally.

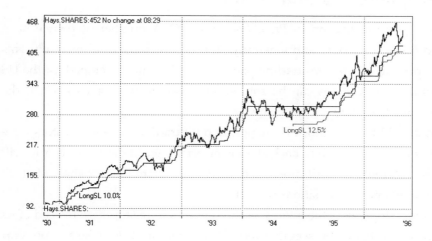

Source: Updata

With Hays 12.5% works a treat.

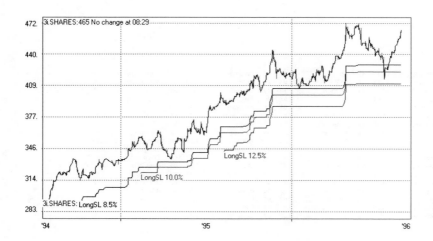

Source: Updata

A rare example where less than 10% worked for the short term investors. Long term investors may choose to ride out the short term falls with a bigger stop-loss.

Using Stop-loss as a Start Profit

This concept was touched on in *Profit from your PC*. A number of people have commented on its originality and ingenuity, so it deserves a second mention. This was really born out of a futures trading package that Updata developed for the US market. Futures and options can be sold short, meaning the right to sell at the current price at a later date.

With the old London Stock Exchange account trading system investors were able to sell at one price and buy back at a lower price later in the account. You will often see the term where institutions or market makers are long or short of stock matching bought and sold positions respectively.

The short stop-loss is the reverse of the standard long stop-loss. Instead of its helping you to cut losses by seeing a move back from a peak, it helps you start profits by showing a reversal from a trough.

At Updata, we call this a start profit. This can be highly useful for traded options traders dealing in put options. Below is a monthly leaders and laggards of the London Traded Options Market underlying shares used to help find some examples.

1	Railtrack	19.14	19	Blue Cir	8.06	37	Courtald	4.28	54	Pru Corp	0.47
2	Barclays	14.73	20	RTZ	7.84	38	GEC	4.14	55=	Ald Domeq	0
3	BSkyB	14.17	21	SKlineB	7.78	39	Asda Grp	3.74	55=	R-Royce	0
4	Lucas	12.09	22	BP	7.63	40	Safeway	3.49	55=	Sears	0
5	Grand Mt	11.53	23	Br Gas	7.61	41	P&O dfd	3.43	56	ICI	-0.06
6	HSBC $	11.41	24	Std Chtd	7.55	42	NatPower	3.31	57	Hanson	-0.32
7	Storehse	10.99	25	Abbey Nt	7.5	43	Glaxo	3.25	58	Cable&W	-1.21
8	Tesco	10.79	26	Br Steel	7.46	44	Cadbury	3.04	59	Tarmac	-1.48
9	Zeneca	10.28	27	Royal & S	7.26	45=	Williams	2.99	60	BAA	-2.02
10	Ladbroke	10.03	28	ThornEMI	7.16	45=	Guinness	2.99	61	ThamesWtr	-2.51
11	Boots	9.44	29	BTR	6.32	46	Orange	2.93	62	Tomkins	-2.68
12	Hillsdwn	9.36	30	PowerGen	6.22	47	M & S	2.82	63	Scot Pwr	-3.21
13	Land Sec	9.28	31	BT	5.65	48	Redland	2.35	64	Lonrho	-4.14
14	NatWest	9.05	32	FTSE	5.25	49	BritAero	2.01	65	Utd Bisc	-5
15	Kingfish	8.55	33	Unilever	5.12	50	Br Air	1.65	66	BAT Inds	-12.02
16	Dixons	8.48	34	LASMO	4.92	51	Pilk'ton	1.56	67	Amstrad	-25.65
17	Vodafone	8.35	35	Reuters	4.35	52	EMI	1.51			
18	Sainsbry	8.3	36	Bass	4.33	53	Com Uni	1.11			

Source: Updata

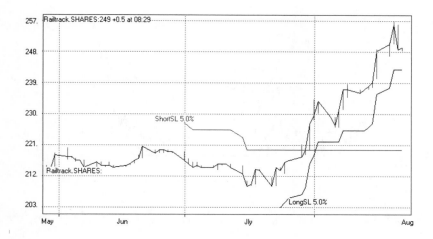

Source: Updata

Stop-losses are ideal when there is a shortage of price history to go on. The start profit gave a signal at a level which may be considered a breakout.

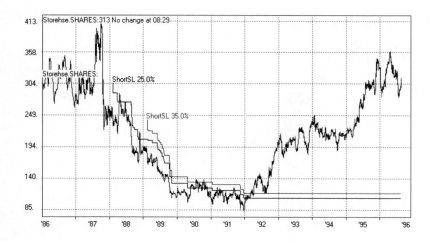

Source: Updata

Here the 35% short stop-loss may have helped you decide there was a turnaround or a start profit.

Source: Updata

Here the 5% or 10% short stop-loss got you in, but this is no match for the trend lines identifying a triangle for the optimum timing.

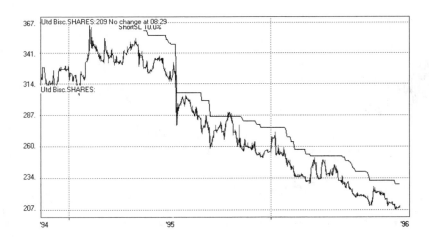

Source: Updata

Here the short stop-loss helps you stay in the put options, or out of the shares.

CHAPTER EIGHT

Short Term Indicators

● ●

In *Profit from your PC* we covered short term indicators briefly under 'Getting More Sophisticated'. This level of analysis is further than I like to go and I am concerned that so many investors who use technical analysis rush to use these tools before using simple ones such as trends and overlays. A brief summary of the main short term indicators follows with some examples.

Short term indicators (STI), or oscillators, are second order indicators. Those who have studied calculus in mathematics will appreciate the significance of this. Short term indicators are derived from first order indicators, such as moving averages.

The best way to get a feel for this is to make an analogy with some elementary physics.

Measurement	— Distance	— Price movement, trend lines, stop-losses
First Order	— Velocity or speed	— Moving Averages
Second Order	— Acceleration	— Momentum, RSI, OBOS, MACD

Short term indicators are really only useful for looking back over a relatively short period of time and short term trading. A good way to think of them is as acceleration and deceleration indicators. To envisage this, imagine taking your foot off the accelerator in your car. You might not notice any change in speed straight away, but you begin to feel a reversal from acceleration forward to acceleration back (deceleration). The reverse is true if you put your foot on the accelerator to speed up. This is the essence of oscillators. They can show a slowing down or speeding up in price behaviour before it becomes readily noticeable on the graph.

Momentum

The momentum of a price line measures, as its name implies, whether the price line is running out of, or gathering, steam. This is where using cycle periods really pays off, because it is calculated as the ratio between the current price and the price of one full cycle ago.

As with other indicators it is necessary to look back and see how the price line changed with previous signals given by the momentum indicator. A quarter and a half cycle length often give good signals, but again it is a case of studying this in an historical context. We are looking for extremes in the graph.

Momentum is normally in one of four states:

1. Positive (ie. above the central axis) and rising; prices are increasing and accelerating (ie. they are increasing more and more quickly).

2. Positive and falling (ie. decelerating); prices are 'still' moving up, but more slowly.

3. Negative and falling; prices are falling more and more rapidly.

4. Negative and rising; prices are 'still' falling but less and less rapidly.

Notice the use of the word 'still', due to the fact that the first and third states must have already occurred, in the second and fourth states respectively. It is the transition between states that is of interest. When momentum crosses the central axis, this implies that the trend has changed direction.

This signal can often be late and it is likely that much of the change has occurred. Momentum tends to change from one extreme to another very rapidly, and often 'lingers' around these extremes. Hence when momentum is on these extremes you need to be looking out for the first sign of a reversal.

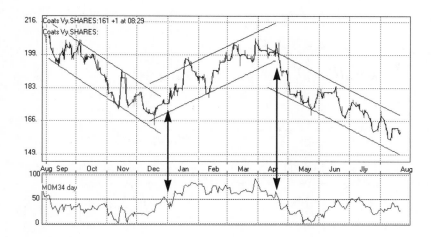

Source: Updata

Coats Vyella have a trough around once a month, so I have used a 34 day momentum. Notice how momentum is negative in the downtrends and positive in the uptrends. A short term strategy of buying when momentum moved positive and selling when moving negative would have worked here.

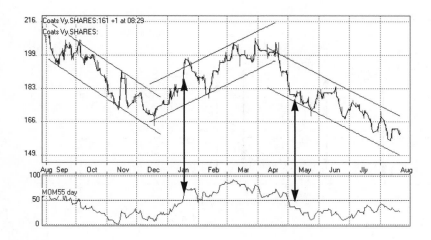

Source: Updata

A 55 day momentum would have given signals too late, which is why the cycle period chosen is so vital.

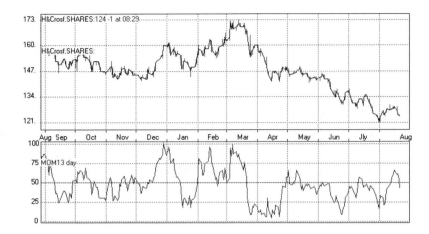

Source: Updata

At first glance, this graph has two troughs a month. This can be dangerous because looking at it more closely these troughs are like double bottoms of the cycle. The cycle pattern is what is important. Placing some trend channels on the graph can help to get a better feel of the cycle as shown below.

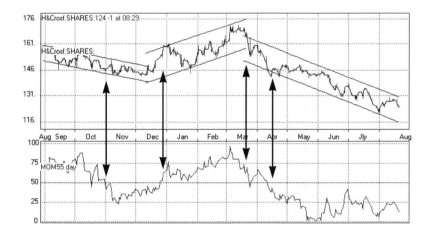

Source: Updata

In the latest channel the price line seems to be on the boundary every two months, so a 55 day momentum is more suitable. The theory is that this downtrend should be over when momentum heads into the top half again.

Relative Strength Indicator (RSI)

The relative strength indicator is in essence a measure of short term momentum, and shows whether the price line is speeding up or slowing down. It is calculated by comparing the average of the falls with the average of the rises within the defined period. It is measured on a percentage scale of 0 to 100 as a rule. When the indicator is below 25 the investment is oversold and when it is above 75 it is overbought.

RSI assists in deciding **when** the price line is overbought or oversold, though some stocks may remain in either state for a very long time. It is effectively a measure of momentum. It is automatically drawn on a percentage scale.

1. The area between 0 and 25% represents oversold

2. The area between 75 and 100% represents overbought

These regions are usually considered critical. Once again, this should be verified historically and adjusted accordingly, as the areas actually are not so rigidly defined. These areas may also change slightly depending on the sort of market conditions that reign generally.

For instance, in a bull market 80 and 30 may be the levels used, while in a bear market 70 and 20 may be more suitable. When the RSI starts to move out of these areas the signal to buy or sell is given.

Hence when RSI is in the extreme bands one should anticipate when it is about to move into the central band. RSI, unlike most other indicators, also works quite well in a sideways market.

Another consideration, often known as the 'divergence factor', is when the price line and RSI are doing different things.

1. A price line scaling new peaks, when RSI is not, is a bad sign and usually indicates that it is time to sell.

2. A price line at new lows, while RSI is not, is a good sign and usually indicates that it is time to buy.

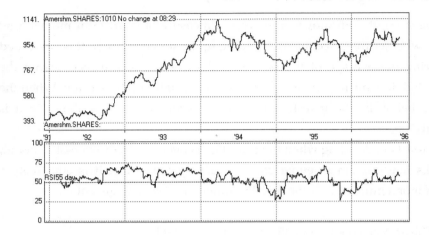

Source: Updata

For this stock RSI never makes it into overbought or oversold territory on the 55 day period.

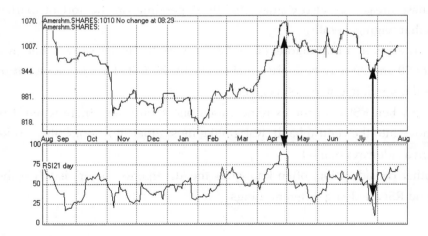

Source: Updata

For the braver short term trader a 21 day RSI gave good signals on the peak and trough.

Overbought/Oversold (OBOS)

This is simply measured by the distance between the price line and its average. It is a useful indicator, as it tells the investor whether something is 'overbought' or 'oversold'. The OBOS line often appears in a cyclical form due to the fact that the average oscillates about the price line. The main points of interest on the graph are the extremes where it starts to turn and especially where it crosses the zero axis which shows the price line is being crossed. This means that a price reversal may be imminent.

OBOS is telling us information about the moving average technique without actually using it. It must be stressed that OBOS falling does not necessarily indicate that the price line is falling.

1. When OBOS crosses the central axis we know that the moving average crosses the price line.

2. When OBOS is near the extremes of the bottom window it is said to be 'overbought' (if near the top) or 'oversold' (near the bottom).

Study what OBOS has done in the past in order to assess where the extremes are. If OBOS is on or near its maximum distance away from the centre line then it is almost certain that this extreme cannot be sustained for very long at all. It is most likely that the price line will come back in line with its average. So, we should be looking for OBOS either 'topping out' in the overbought area or 'bottoming out' in the oversold area with a reversal in the other direction beginning to occur.

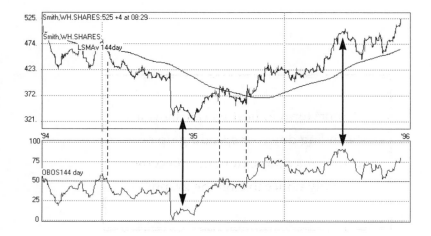

Source: Updata

In the graph on page 119 the dotted lines show where the price line crosses the moving average (ie. the distance is zero), the solid lines show the overbought and oversold regions where the price line is furthest from its average. You need to look for the point where OBOS is starting to turn from these extremes. It is also useful to look back at the OBOS line historically to put a high level or divergence into context.

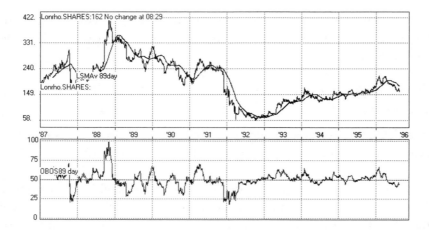

Source: Updata

OBOS used to work well for Lonrho. It highlighted the low in 1992 where the 89 day moving average gave a clear signal. Its smoother performance since has made it less suitable.

> "Short term indicators can show a slowing down or speeding up of price behaviour before they become readily noticeable on the graph."

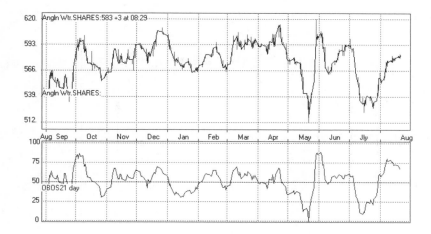

Source: Updata

Short term traders may have used a 21 day OBOS to get in and out of Anglian Water recently.

Moving Average Convergence/Divergence (MACD)

This graph comes from the second method of using moving averages. It measures the distance between two averages of different periods and is again used to spot divergence. It is similar to the overbought/oversold indicator in appearance and is also drawn on the same type of scale. Again, when this graph crosses the zero axis a 'buy' or 'sell' signal is given.

Like OBOS, MACD shows the distance between two lines (this time two moving averages) which is not always readily apparent just by looking at them. Use a full cycle period as the averaging length of the first moving average and a shorter period for the second. The short period is like a smoothed version of the price line.

1. When MACD crosses the central axis this means that the two moving averages are crossing each other and either a 'golden cross' or a 'dead cross' is occurring.

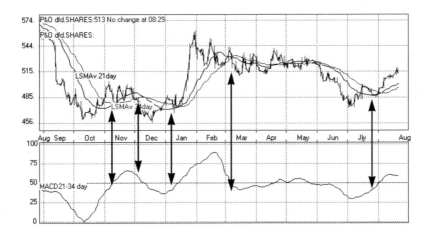

Source: Updata

A cross through the central axis indicates the averages have crossed. MACD doesn't always tell you whether the crosses between the averages are golden or dead crosses. A decisive cut through the central axis (30 or 45 degrees) is normally a good indication of the validity of the cross.

Stochastics

The last of the short term indicators is a group of functions called the stochastics. These are sometimes used in probability and statistics. They assume that prices on the price line accumulate near the peaks of uptrends and the troughs of downtrends, as does the data near the reversal points in a cycle. Therefore for this analysis to be effective the price history should follow a clear cycle or behave in a defined trend channel. Like the other short term indicators, these functions employ cycle periods. Basically the main stochastic function relates the current price to its relative position within the averaging period chosen. This function can then be averaged to produce lines much the same as in averages. 'Buy' and 'Sell' signals are given by these graphs in a similar manner to the analysis which uses moving averages of different averaging periods.

The main stochastic function relates the current price to its relative position within the averaging period. Another two graphs are automatically drawn with the stochastic graph. The first is a three day moving average of the stochastic, known as a K curve. The second is a three day moving average of the K curve, known as a D curve. These act as a smoothing measure and, as the averaging period implies, are best for short term trading.

A simple analysis is as follows:

1. 'Bullish' divergence occurs where the price line falls to new lows while K moves upwards. The decision to buy is given when the K curve moves up through the stochastic line.

2. 'Bearish divergence' is where the price line reaches new peaks but the K curve does not. The sell signal is given on the day the K curve crosses down through the stochastic line.

After a strong rise or fall the price line often consolidates, away from the extreme values. Once the stochastics start moving in the opposite directions, a price reversal is imminent. Stochastics also show overbought and oversold at the extremes.

The 'double smoothing' effect of the D curve can be utilised to avoid 'whiplash' effects removing erratic fluctuations present in the analysis using the stochastic curve and K. The analysis is the same except K now takes the place of the stochastic curve and D takes the place of K. Basically buy signals are given when K rises above D and sell signals when K moves below D.

Stochastics can be useful for short term trading in the trend channel. The price line often turns before or after the boundaries and stochastics can show this clearly.

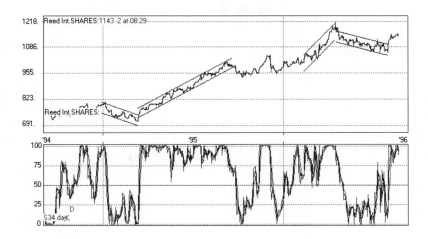

Source: Updata

The stochastic runs along the top of its range in an uptrend and the bottom in a downtrend. It is quick to identify this change in trend as it moves from the top half to the bottom half.

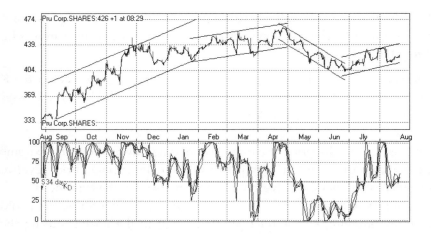

Source: Updata

To feel comfortable with stochastics, you need to see them staying within one half. When the trend is sideways the indicator is not very useful. Notice how it stays in the top half in the uptrend and the bottom half in the downtrend again. It helps to identify the end of a short trend which is often difficult.

CHAPTER NINE

Looking at some graphs twelve months on

● ●

In receiving feedback for *Profit from your PC* a small number of readers pointed out that I had the benefit of hindsight in choosing graphs as examples. I empathise with this, which is precisely why we developed the Profit stockmarket simulation game at Updata. The idea was that people could practise buying and selling shares on real life examples and hopefully get better at spotting reversals.

In this chapter we look at some of the examples and how the graphs have changed since. This is by no means an 'I told you so', just simply an illustration of what can happen, after some signals have been given.

The graph at the top of each page is a copy of the relevant example and its page number and caption used in *Profit from your PC*, while the one below it is the more up to date graph which shows the new picture including the last year of data.

I have selected the examples that I found most interesting in order to keep the book size manageable. Those people who have a software package might find it useful to go through this review exercise on their PC. The graphs will be more up to date and you can place the analysis on yourself.

> "It is useful to look back at the criteria on which you based your investment decisions. Has the picture changed?"

Source: Updata

Page 25 – 'it seems a fair assumption that over the period this line is close to the true value of the share'.

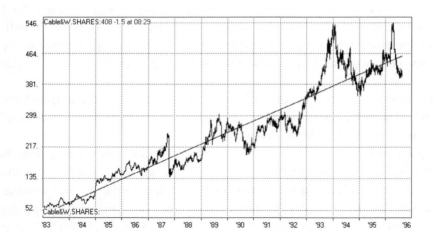

Source: Updata

The oscillation either side of this central line continues.

Source: Updata

Page 65 – BP with an auto-trend channel showing general trend.

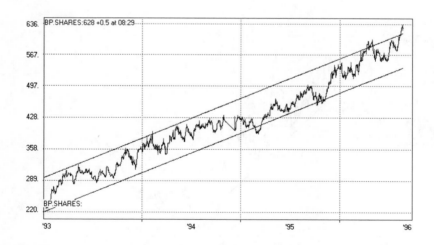

Source: Updata

The trend continues.

Source: Updata

Page 79 – Asda drifts sideways out of the downward trend channel, and takes another two years to fully turn and break out.

Source: Updata

Asda keeps rising.

Source: Updata

Page 105 – Blue Circle has a lot of lost ground to make up.

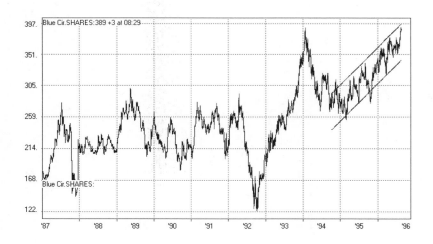

Source: Updata

The trend continues.

Source: Updata

Page 106 – British Aerospace also recovers in 1993.

Source: Updata

Depending on how you look at it, either the trend is breached or the trend steepens.

Source: Updata

Page 107 – Carlton recovers in 1991.

Source: Updata

The trend continues.

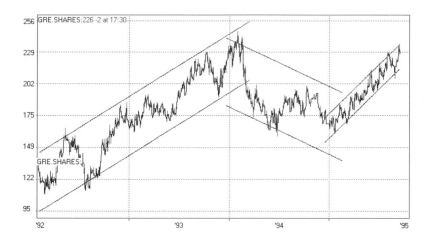

Source: Updata

Page 108 – Guardian Royal Insurance start trading in a more predictable trend channel at the beginning of 1995.

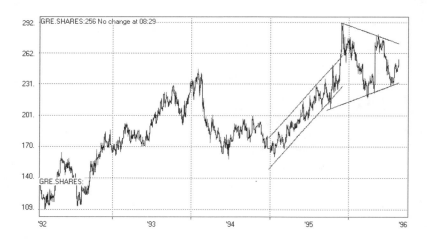

Source: Updata

Then a move up through the trend, leading to less predictable behaviour which is being damped into a sideways triangle – wait for the breakout or breakdown.

Source: Updata

Page 110 – Enterprise Oil starting to trade sideways out of trend.

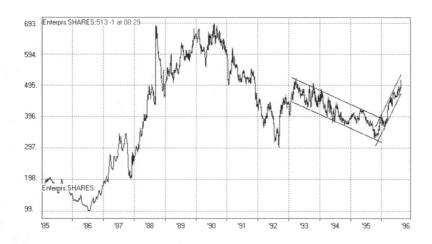

Source: Updata

The upturn comes soon after.

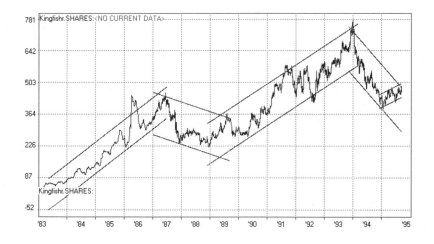

Source: Updata

Page 111 – Kingfisher, a new trend building, will it win this time?

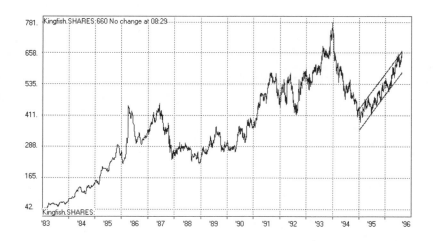

Source: Updata

The trend wins and continues.

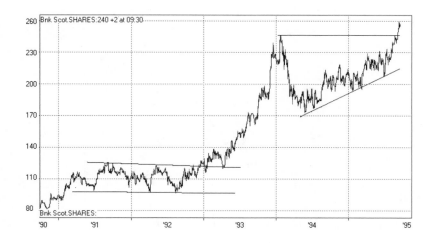

Source: Updata

Page 115 – Bank of Scotland breaking into new territory again.

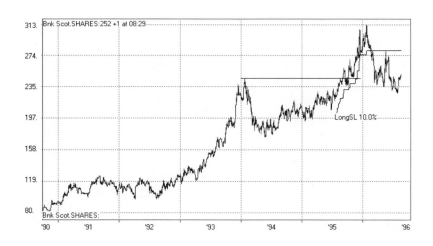

Source: Updata

Broke into new territory for a short run with a 20% profit protected by stop-loss.

Source: Updata

Page 117 – M&S – very well behaved.

Source: Updata

Business as usual.

Source: Updata

Page 117 – Lloyds – a tight trading range.

Source: Updata

Still a tight trading range, but even steeper.

Source: Updata

Page 118 – Shell – no slippery slopes.

Source: Updata

Still no slippery slopes.

Source: Updata

Page 119 – Scottish & Newcastle is one of the best trending stocks there is. Great for worry free investment.

Source: Updata

Still worry free long term. At the top of its trading range short term.

Source: Updata

Page 119 – Tate & Lyle are also well behaved.

Source: Updata

Very well behaved, nearing the bottom of the trend channel.

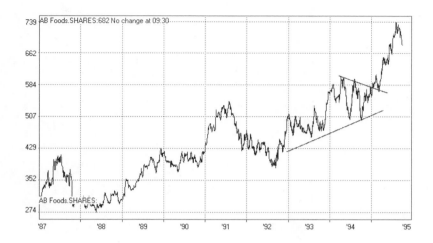

Source: Updata

Page 120 – AB Foods – experience big sudden falls in 1994, and sudden recoveries, twice, before running again.

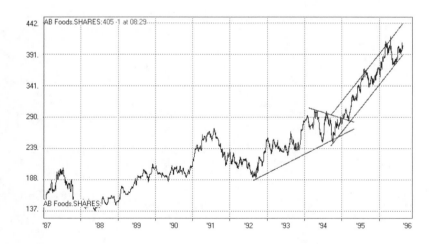

Source: Updata

Running still further, and now displaying more predictable behaviour.

Source: Updata

Page 132 – Guinness – change direction to sideways in 1992.

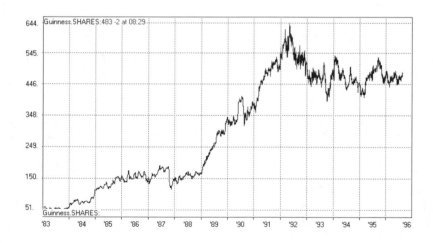

Source: Updata

And still sideways.

Source: Updata

Page 133 – Hanson – looks like the end of this long run in 1995.

Source: Updata

Understatement of the year.

Source: Updata

Page 133 – Inchcape – falls through two levels in 1994 and 1995.

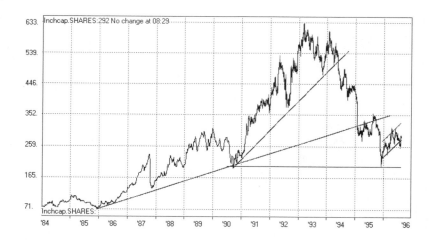

Source: Updata

And tries one last time in 1996. The problem is that long term support has been breached. It will need to get above this support level again to be confident of a recovery.

I hope this chapter serves as a useful review. Those who are lucky enough to have graphing software with automated collection can look at each of these examples and many other stocks in the market under constant and on-going review.

CHAPTER TEN

A technical approach for small companies

• •

Private investors frequently ask me to comment on the graphs of small companies. I often shy away from this on the basis that they are normally higher risk. While spectacular returns are possible, investors need to understand they are playing with fire. The other problem is that the graphs of smaller companies behave less predictably because there is much less trading volume. Efficiency of markets is greatly increased with trading volume along with liquidity of the shares and the resulting spread between buy and sell prices. Over 90% of UK trading volume occurs in the top 1,000 stocks out of the near 3,000 shares on the London Stock Exchange. Consequently, the smallest 250 shares will show a vast variation in performance compared to the top 250 shares. **Check liquidity first. Shares that are hard to buy while rising may be twice as hard to sell when falling. Don't get into a share if you can't get out when you want to.**

Having started and grown a small technology company, I am aware of the considerably different risk-reward profile that smaller companies present. I am often reminded that private investors don't always appreciate how differently shares in smaller companies behave.

In this chapter we take a brief look at some examples of small companies. The examples are chosen from the recently created Alternative Investment Market using a leaders and laggards search.

Price movement in small companies tends to fall into two camps:

- Flat and sideways with little activity
- Dramatic in either direction

The excitement starts when small companies go through the transition from the former to the latter behaviour. The problem with this is that it is very difficult to predict when a company whose shares have traded sideways for some time will start to move up. Small companies can become very long term investments and in many cases will never produce a return.

If you want to get in at the ground level, then a fundamental analysis approach is probably more suitable. Building an understanding of the people behind the business and their vision will be much more helpful.

This is another skill set. A technical approach may be to look for companies where the share price is starting to increase dramatically.

Whatever you decide from the graph, it will be well worth a second analysis with some more fundamental information from your broker or a good look at the company's annual report.

You may miss the first bit of the rise or even miss the boat altogether, but it ensures that your money isn't tied up in companies that are not going somewhere. Investors often forget to take a 20% rise in one year and divide it by the five years they have held the stock.

Another key characteristic of price behaviour in small companies is that a steep rise is often short lived. Many shares give up the substantial gains they have made and fall back again very quickly.

What goes up quickly can come down quickly, due to crowd behaviour.

The expectation is invariably bigger than the event. With an absence of clear technical signals due to less predicable price behaviour and less history, the stop-loss indicator comes into its own with this kind of investment.

#			#			#			#		
1	PanAndn.R	33.72	41	Norcityll	5.38	64=	Lottrykng	0	87=	Dawson H.	-4.48
2	Toad	30.14	42	AskCentrl	5.26	64=	Manx&Osea	0	88	Cafe Inns	-4.62
3	Antonov	29.09	43	Pet City	4.93	64=	ParkEst.L	0	89	ThomasPts	-4.76
4	EpicMltrnd	28.17	44	SouthnNws	4.76	64=	PrimryHth	0	90	La Senza	-4.83
5	AshurstTc	27.78	45	AbacusRec	4.65	64=	PrismRail	0	91	NECAHldgs	-5.56
6	AfrcnGold	25	46	SuryFrlnn	4.53	64=	RaphaelZH	0	92=	Omnimedia	-5.88
7	ANDIntPub	23.61	47	DBSMngmnt	4.05	64=	RevltnPlc	0	92=	Ricemnlns	-5.88
8	Cardcast	22.86	48	West175En	4	64=	RushmreWW	0	93	OptclCare	-6.19
9	Moorepay	18.69	49	CircleCom	3.43	64=	SEAMultim	0	94	PordurnFds	-6.25
10	VDC	18.42	50	NeillClrk	3.03	64=	Scotswdln	0	95	Easynet	-6.45
11	Waterfall	17.39	51	HydroDynm	2.61	64=	SiraBsnsS	0	96	Flomerics	-6.67
12	DigtlAnim	15.38	52	Nash(Wi.)	2.56	64=	Tradepnt.	0	97=	Dean Corp	-7.69
13	PolymscPh	13.93	53	SolidStSu	2.41	64=	Watermark	0	97=	RushmereW	-7.69
14	Gander H.	13.64	54	Romtec	2.33	64=	WestnSelW	0	98	IntellEnv	-7.89
15	BATMAdvCrn	13.28	55	CarisbkSh	2.15	64=	Whitecrss	0	99	Hat Pin	-7.94
16	Albrmle&B	11.76	56	AnnStBrew	2.13	64=	Winchestr	0	100	Systmslnt	-7.95
17	Hansom Gp	11.11	57	Mulberry	2	65	Caledonia	-0.53	101	Theo Fenn	-8.79
18	Scott Pic	10.81	58	Omnicare	1.85	66	NursngHmP	-0.88	102	HerculesP	-9.09
19	Mountcshl	10.53	59	AMCO Corp	1.79	67	Fibernet	-0.9	103	NorthnPet	-9.43
20	TRACKRNet	10.31	60	Freepages	1.59	68	Prestn.NE	-0.95	104	IndpndEgy	-9.47
21	XavierCpr	10	61	SCiEntGrp	1.23	69	SinclrMon	-1.15	105	Marine&M.	-11.11
22	Chartwlll	9.23	62	Brockbank	1.07	70	UNO	-1.19	106	Stentor	-11.89
23	Cirqual	9.16	63	FurlngHrns	0.74	71	Scruttons	-1.64	107	AlphaOmkn	-14.29
24	Ballyntry	9.09	64=	Belcanto	0	72	JenningsB	-1.69	108	Multimdia	-14.75
25	Trocadero	8.45	64=	CardClear	0	73	KSBiomedx	-2.15	109	Actvlmgng	-15.94
26	CCI	8.33	64=	CavdshWte	0	74	IndontRad	-2.31	110	NeilsnCob	-18.07

Source: Updata

A monthly leaders and laggards on the AIM listed shares. Notice the high proportion of shares that have not changed compared to two stocks in the FT-SE 100 (see Introduction).

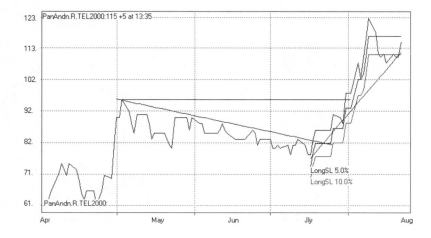

Source: Updata

With little history to go on, could we have spotted the recovery through the first trend or the breakout into new territory? Having seen a ten per cent stop-loss already breached for a short time, 12.5% might be better.

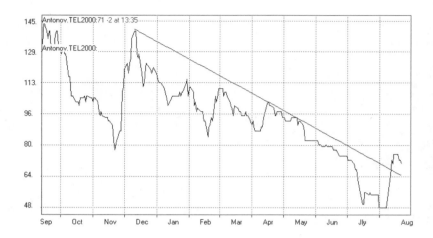

Source: Updata

Recoveries are much more risky with smaller companies, as there is more scope for the shares to be worthless than in bigger companies. More reason to confirm trending behaviour as much as possible. If in doubt, wait for the breakout.

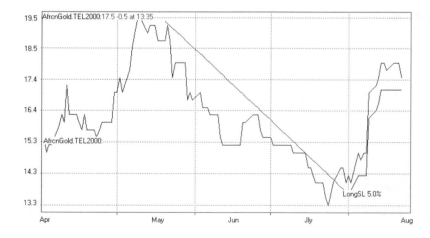

Source: Updata

Sharp rises like this are easy to miss. The 90/10 rule again – 90% of the time deciding where the share price should be, 10% getting there.

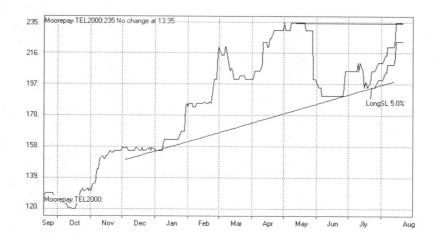

Source: Updata

Having trouble breaking out, or a triangle? Seems to be more predictable than most smaller company shares.

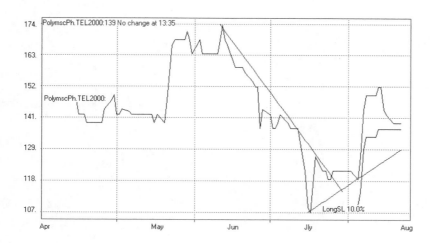

Source: Updata

Don't ever forget that this share is capable of falling by 40 per cent in a few weeks.

Source: Updata

Low priced shares, what is the upside?

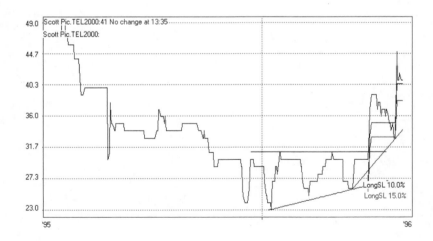

Source: Updata

Even 15% stop-loss may not be enough. Can this stock double as easily as it halved?

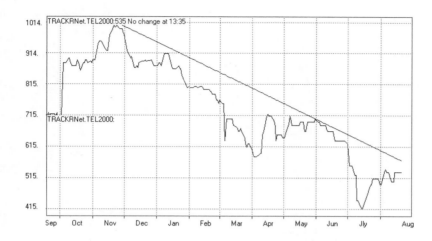

Source: Updata

A well publicised company, the reality is it hasn't performed well.

What goes up, often comes down – the pitfalls

Source: Updata

One of the greatest success stories on AIM becomes one of the greatest disasters. Not much time to get in, plenty of time to get out. People find it very difficult emotionally to sell at 10% or 20% from the top and even more difficult at 40% or 60%.

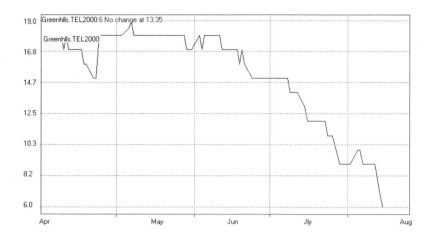

Source: Updata

Surely it can't fall lower than 10p. Don't forget: 10p to 6p is worse than 100p to 60p or £10 to £6, when less favourable spreads (difference between Buy and Sell price) are taken into account.

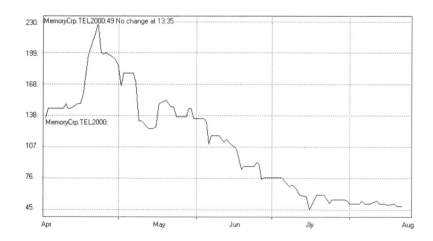

Source: Updata

A stockmarket darling when floated turns to disaster.

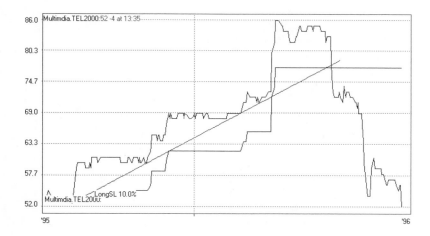

Source: Updata

There are also countless examples of small fully listed companies to look at and a monthly leaders and laggards on the whole market helps to unearth them.

◆ ◆ ◆

CHAPTER ELEVEN

The changing world for PC based investors

* *

Profit from your PC contained chapters on computers, getting data, software and the Internet. The Internet has become such an integral part of home computing and will become so critical for the PC based investor, that I have dedicated a whole part of this book to the subject. In this chapter we look at PCs, data collection and investment software, enlarging what was covered in the previous book.

Computers

In the last year PCs have become much more powerful and fallen still further in price. Previously I had advised that the uninitiated should be able to pick up a personal computer that is more than adequate for several hundred pounds. You can now acquire the same level of PC for even less, but so much value for money now exists at several hundred pounds or for higher specifications at just over one thousand pounds that these price points are well worth consideration.

The front runners in the UK, at the time of writing, for value (performance and features versus price) seem to have narrowed to Dell and Gateway. I am increasingly astonished at what you can get for your money. This is quite off-putting for many would-be PC purchasers. You need to take the plunge sooner or later. Buying a new PC is a bit like buying a new car. You will probably want to replace it every few years. I am now finding that my buying cycle has been reduced from every couple of years to every year for a new PC. The increased performance at reduced prices is simply too good to miss.

If you are switching on your new PC every day and finding that you are becoming frustrated at waiting, give upgrading some thought. If you have upgraded before you will probably remember the joy of increased speed, bar a few teething troubles. I now budget £1,500 annually, less than five pounds a day, for the difference between enjoying my PC and telling it to hurry up all the time.

In the UK, Dixon's PC World has become the clear market leader for retail PC purchasing. Going and having a test drive on a number of different machines at one of these superstores is recommended if you are not sure about what you want. If you are, ordering direct over the telephone with Dell or Gateway is fairly safe. You may well do best to get quotations from both. Their free-phone numbers are listed in advertisements in all the main PC magazines. It is worth comparing their prices in the ads and over the phone as well as having the relevant ads in front of you so you can understand what PC the salesperson at the other end of the line is talking about.

An update to the general rules given in *Profit from your PC* follows:

1. Buy the top of the range rather than the bottom. A Pentium 133 or 166 is probably better value than a Pentium Pro 200, the low end of the next level up.

2. Get as big a hard disk as you can afford. You will probably fill it up eventually no matter how big it is. Over 1 Gigabyte (1,000 Megabytes) is recommended.

3. The more memory (RAM) you have, the faster your programs will run. 16 MB is increasingly becoming a minimum and if you want more enjoyment 32MB is worth it. Memory chips have more than halved in the past year, making this element now much more affordable.

4. Get a CD-Rom if you can afford it, as this format is becoming the standard. These are now such an affordable add-on with six and eight speed drives coming in at under £100.

5. Choose Microsoft Windows 95 or NT as your operating system. It is the easiest to use and nearly all quality software packages run on it.

6. Buy a modem. On-line services and 'plug and play' easy to use communications software (no more lengthy configuration sessions) is set to explode. A PC that is not connected will soon be like having a car without wheels.

7. If you want a teletext downloading capability and don't want to install a circuit card yourself later, get one fitted when you buy your machine. WinTV is the

most popular at the time of writing and we at Updata work very closely with this manufacturer.

8. Make sure the machine you buy comes with a minimum of one year's on-site warranty. If it comes with this kind of guarantee then you almost certainly will not have problems. Those who are completely PC illiterate may opt for an extended warranty of two or three years.

9. Unless you really know your stuff, buy a brand of PC which is made by a large and reputable manufacturer. Normally they will have won a number of awards from the PC press.

10. View your PC purchase as a bit like buying a car. How long can you reasonably expect to use it for, before upgrading to the next model?

Getting Data

Previously I outlined four main methods of getting data into your PC.

1. Manual entry

2. Disk and CD-Rom

3. TV and Satellite broadcast

4. Modem – on-line services

Manual entry has really gone by the wayside. Data input has to be one of the most boring tasks known to man. Avoid it from day one if you can. If you are still doing it you probably won't have much time left to follow your investments.

Disk and CD-Rom

Most disk services have been superseded by on-line services. A year ago I had high hopes for CD-Rom for investors. With the 650 Megabyte capacity and fairly low production costs, CDs seemed the ideal medium for databases of companies and historical data. It appears, however, that the Internet is replacing this, though it will be some time before the Net has anything like the kind of speed of transfer of high volumes of data. CDs are great for multimedia and annually updated encyclopaedias but are not much use for data that is changing by the hour, minute or second.

TV and Satellite Broadcast

In the UK these services fall into two main categories:

1. Teletext services

2. Real time services

Teletext Services

The main services in the UK offering financial information are BBC2 Ceefax and Channel 4 Teletext. SkyText on the Sky satellite service is increasingly worth looking at as well.

The services offer the top 400 shares six times a day, currencies, indices and commodities. The London Stock Exchange limits these broadcasts in terms of number of shares and frequency of broadcast. For data services that go beyond these limits, the LSE levies exchange fees just short of £200 per annum. Some on-line services are building this into a pay as you go structure.

Channel 4 Teletext offers all UK prices from midnight, which serves as an ideal way of keeping charts up to date. This service was born out of a joint venture between Updata and Teletext, and Updata's Teleshares package was designed to help PC based investors utilise the service.

Teletext and the PC

You can get the prices from teletext into your PC with a special circuit card which goes inside the machine. This can be a teletext only card or PC/TV card which allows your PC to display live television in a window. Once you have installed the card, simply plug a TV aerial into the back of your machine and you are on-line with no on-line costs.

Now all you need is some fairly straightforward software which will communicate with the teletext circuit card and download the prices and store them to your PC's hard disk. Once these prices are stored day after day you can graph the history. Updata gives away years of price history with its software packages so that people have some useful history to start with.

With a TV card you can watch live television while your software collects and stores teletext information.

Real Time Data Feeds

There are a few services in the UK delivered over data broadcast on terrestrial TV and satellite.

At Updata we spend our lives talking to a number of information providers of various sizes. At the moment real time prices on the whole UK market will cost around £1,000 a year. The challenge will be for an information vendor to offer prices at a much more affordable price level. We expect that with competing Internet services, real time prices on all UK equities will be available within a year at around £500 per annum.

Market-Eye

The most established real time equities service for the private investor in the UK is Market-Eye. This was previously run by the London Stock Exchange itself, but was taken up by ICV a few years ago. Market-Eye now comes in two ways:

1. The Black Box Market-Eye Terminal

2. PC Market-Eye circuit card and Windows software

While the Market-Eye service is unlikely to fall in price in the foreseeable future, it seems as if it will remain the most comprehensive service, in terms of content and reliability, for some time. At the time of writing a new PC Market-Eye news service is being released. ICV also have plans to expand the service in other ways.

PC Market-Eye comes with some basic price display software, shown below. But the real benefit is the ability for third party software applications to store this information and produce graphs. Because the data is real time, these graphs can show every single change in price. This is covered in depth in the *Getting More Advanced* section in Part Two of this book.

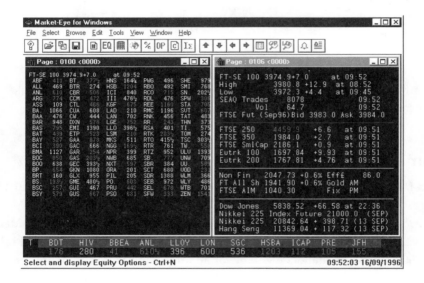

PC Market-Eye for Windows gives a window on the market, but doesn't save any of the incoming data.

Satellite Services

Another service for private investors to consider is Tenfore. Its main advantage is that it covers a whole range of markets world-wide. This is especially useful for those who wish to follow US markets. Signal, a US based data feed, is also making inroads into the UK.

Modems

A few years ago most people didn't know what a modem was. The massive awareness that the Internet has created has meant that they are becoming standard with most new PCs. For those who are still in the dark, a modem links your PC to on-line services via a normal telephone line. This book has a whole section on the Internet, where there is a vast range of services. Here we look at some non-Internet based services in the UK.

On-line services for UK investors (Non-Internet)

Many on-line services over the past few years have involved the user in protracted comms (short for communications) setup and keystroke commands not too dissimilar to using MS-DOS. The usability improvements are driving on-line services into the mainstream.

Infotrade

This company was set up by Mitsubishi Electric of Japan who bought out the UK computer manufacturer, Apricot. Infotrade has been heavily promoted in the national press, so most readers will know about it. It comes on CD-Rom and thereafter offers a range of services on-line. There are some interesting areas covered by the product including on-line dealing and portfolio management, news and fundamental company data. The main disadvantage of the service is that, because it is not offered over the Internet, the cost of the call is at a national rate unless you live in the Birmingham area. Infotrade are now offering Internet access, via their service. Clearly the company is taking a long term view of the UK private investor market, looking at the size of their promotional budget. Infotrade and ESI (See Internet) appear to have been fighting it out to gain the major share of the potential on-line UK investor market.

CompuServe

CompuServe is one of the biggest on-line services in the world, with millions of users world-wide of which a few hundred thousand are in the UK. Being on CompuServe costs a standard $9.95 per month with a series of premium services for which you pay more. CompuServe software is easy to use with a selection of intuitive icons for users to click on. A number of investment related topics and forums are covered on CompuServe, though there is often a US slant even within the UK dedicated areas.

Prestel On-line

Prestel, based in London, started its life as a BT service but has since become independent. Prestel On-line also has a number of Internet developments which are covered in Part Three. Prestel have been quite clever to offer a different level of on-line information depending on what type of investor you are. They offer the following services:

1. Free Citifeed service – closing mid prices after midnight (previous day), downloaded in 15 seconds. This is a compressed file which can be unzipped on your PC. See Internet Section.

2. Citifeed service – all UK mid prices from 6.30pm – Cost £75 p.a.

3. Citifeed Plus – Opening price, closing and high and low and volume, commonly known as OHLCV. Available from midnight. Cost £49 p.a.

4. Citifeed Plus – Opening price, closing and high and low and volume, commonly known as OHLCV. Available from 6.30 pm. Cost £125 p.a.

5. Citifeed Premium offers all the above, plus on-screen access to all UK shares and gilts. Cost £300 p.a. including exchange fees. The main drawback here is the cost of long phone calls and an inability to look at the market as a whole.

It is fairly straightforward to import these prices into most investment software packages.

CIX (Compulink Information Exchange)

An on-line forum that has a wealth of topics discussed by users. The Investment forum is particularly active. Some people seem to live on it. A number of product experiences and views are shared on this medium.

Software

Software is the lifeblood of computers. Without it they are useless lumps of metal with some smatterings of silicon. When we show people our programs they often think that it is incredible what a computer can do. I remind them that the PC is only part of it. People sometimes begrudge paying hundreds of pounds for a disk containing software. The programs on these disks often take many man years to develop and refine. They are constructed around a knowledge base built up over years.

Added to this is the fact that every couple of years mainstream software companies need to go back to the drawing board, to build a new framework that takes advantage of the latest technology. It is a constant process of obsoleting your own products to make sure somebody else doesn't. Our software programs are better than anything I ever dreamed of in the days I was typing data into slow PCs and spending countless hours analysing it. Having the ability, while producing this book, to click on another program, scan the market and then double click on some figures to select some graphs to copy and paste into the word-processed document in a couple of seconds, feels like pure magic at times.

Here we cover software under the following sections:

1. Operating Systems

2. Word Processors, Spreadsheets and Databases

3. Data collection and Feed Integration

4. Price Display Software

5. Graphing Software

6. Portfolio Management

Operating Systems

Operating systems for the IBM compatible (Intel based PC) are now almost entirely the domain of Microsoft. Operating systems are described below.

MS-DOS

DOS has been proclaimed dead for some time but has survived longer than most people expected. If you have old DOS programs you wish to run, fine, but the 'DOS is faster' argument doesn't hold true these days. DOS programs can be run fine in a DOS window under the operating systems that follow.

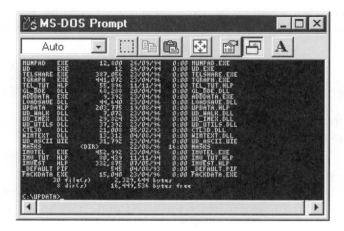

An MS-DOS screen in a window. DOS required the user to learn lots of keystrokes and commands, making it un-user friendly to most of us.

Windows 3.x

There were several versions of the original Microsoft Windows operating system, but the main releases were Windows 3.1 and Windows 3.11 (Windows for Workgroups). Windows was such a revolutionary idea to us at Updata, when we first saw it, that we virtually stopped all our DOS development to build a range of programs that ran on it. It was a decision we never looked back on.

The concept of Windows was that the PC user could run a number of programs, simultaneously, in different Windows allowing him to flip from one application to another. Things have gone a lot further since that original idea, but millions of PC users still happily use Windows today.

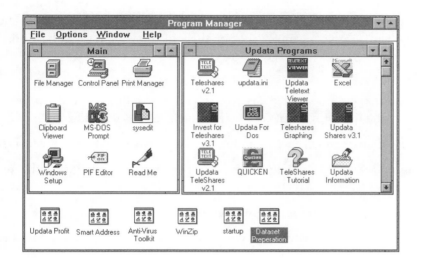

A Windows 3.1 screen now looks quite dated.

One of the big benefits which people often forget with Windows is the ability to refer to on-screen help in one window to assist with an activity in another.

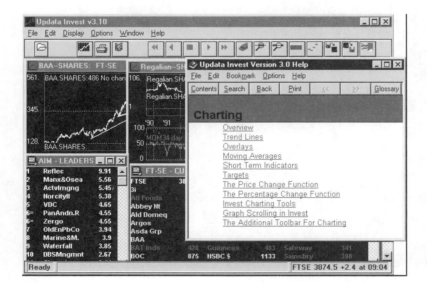

On-screen help in another window (page 165) lets you find the answers you need as you go. Notice the multiple windows within the main graphing application. Windows gave PC users the freedom to look at a number of things at once and swap between them. Users can simply click on the topic they want to get help on.

Windows 95

Much hyped a year ago, Windows 95 has now settled in so happily that it is difficult to know what all the fuss was about. The main benefits of this upgrade are:

1. The interface is much easier and intuitive to use, especially for new users.

2. 'Plug and Play' technology means your system copes better with new devices.

3. It is faster, providing greater productivity.

4. Multitasking means while you wait in one program, you can do things in others.

Many people didn't upgrade to Windows 95 for fear of new instability. It has to be said that, while not as robust as Windows NT, Windows 95 is a big improvement on Windows 3.x. The main drawback is you really need a minimum 486DX with 8MB Ram to run it, but this is now considered a low specification system.

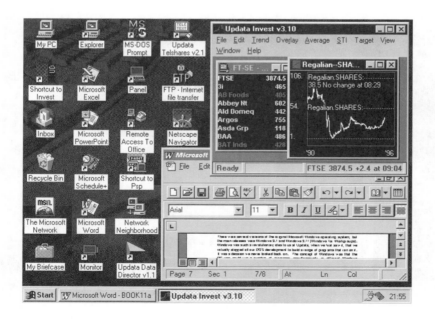

The look and feel of Windows 95 and the desktop environment are also more intuitive. For those still running Windows, Windows 95 is well worth the upgrade.

Windows NT

Windows NT has recently been released in its fourth version and many PC industry commentators say it is the operating system that Windows 95 should have been. Microsoft have been developing this as part of the journey towards their next generation of operating system code-named Cairo. NT now looks like Windows 95, but is more robust and faster. It is a full blown 32 bit operating system which has been developed from the ground up. This is for the serious power user. If you are spending more than £2,000 on a PC, Windows NT Version 4 is worth consideration.

Word Processors, Spreadsheets, Databases

Wordperfect, Lotus and Borland used to be the market leaders in each of these fields respectively. Microsoft have now won the battle in all three categories with Word, Excel and Access. These programs are now most commonly purchased in a 'suite' known as Microsoft Office. The look and feel of these programs is much the same throughout and the ability to share data between them helps you get the most out of them.

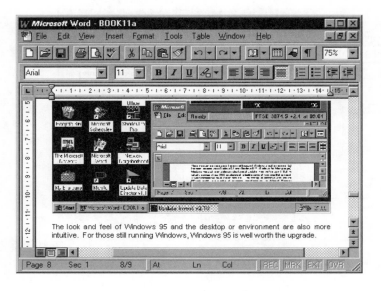

Microsoft Word has a capability way in excess of specialist high end systems used by big companies a few years ago. The whole of this book was written using Word.

Spreadsheets

The spreadsheet remains one of the most ingenious software programs ever invented. First developed by a group of US academics, Visicalc was the first spreadsheet in the world. It was the primary factor in driving rapid sales of the Apple home computer. Suddenly small companies had the level of accounting functionality previously reserved for the big corporations.

The spreadsheet is an essential tool for business these days. Projections and budgets can be produced and amended very easily. Investors will also find this very useful. A high percentage of Updata customers use spreadsheets to track the performance and value of their portfolio. We supply a sample template with all our programs, which is shown below. The results in each cell are produced via the preceding cells and formulas. The prices are linked in live from data collection software via Windows DDE (Dynamic Data Exchange), saving the user the hassle of entering prices to keep the spreadsheet up to date.

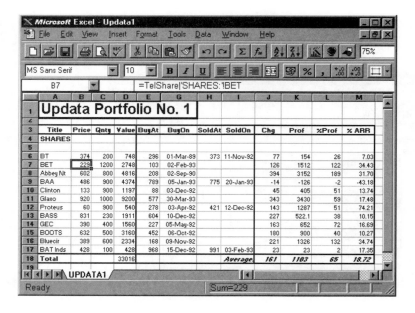

This spreadsheet is fed prices live (column B) via Windows DDE.

Databases

Spreadsheets are in effect a form of database. Databases come into their own when you have a large amount of data to deal with. They allow you to query and search records. Updata's programs are essentially proprietary databases that save the user the complexity of doing these things. Using databases properly will take a little learning for most users but some may find it rewarding. On the whole investors should manage for some time without carrying out their own database development.

Datafeed handling software

Getting data into investment software has traditionally been a nightmare for most PC users. This is changing along with so many aspects of software usability. At Updata we have developed a new generation of data handling software which allows users to choose, on screen, the data source from which they wish to receive data. This also lets users configure what data they would like to receive. Updata is integrating new data sources that come on to the market all the time, including services on the Internet, so that users can easily take advantage of this new data. This data-feed handling software even allows users to collect prices from multiple sources simultaneously.

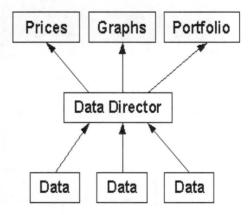

Under the Feeds menu in the Updata Data Director, users can choose which data source they wish to collect data from. This is the engine that does all the work in the background for the software applications that utilise the data.

Price Display Software

When Updata produced its first graphing products, they also included quote screens. Other charting packages didn't do this. We always felt that screens of graphs were more useful if you had price screens to go with them. We took this a step further by allowing users to double click on the price in order to get the graph. Quote screens look fairly straightforward, but we are finding with the latest software technology they can be given a level of usability that even City traders wouldn't have dreamed of.

This is an example of price display software running on teletext.

> "Software is the lifeblood of computers.
> Without it they are useless lumps of
> metal with some smatterings of silicon."

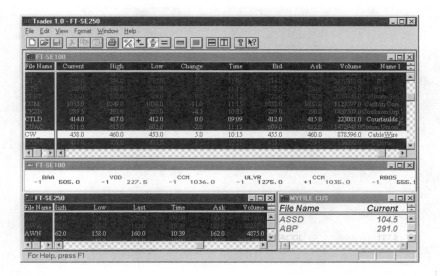

This new price display software, above, can receive data from a range of data sources via the Data Director. You can also look at a range of fields, ie. Bid, Ask, Volume. You can create custom tickers allowing you to view only the changes you wish to see. These custom windows can be created by clicking on a price and dragging it to another window.

Graphing Packages (Charting)

This type of software, traditionally called charting software, is produced by a few companies in the UK and the US. There is little scope to review them here, as they are changing all the time and I'm unlikely to be objective. The main providers in the UK are Synergy and Updata.

There are other companies which advertise from time to time in the investment press. The main function of these programs is to enable the user to carry out the bulk of the technical analysis techniques covered in this book. A few rules for buying investment software appear at the end of this chapter.

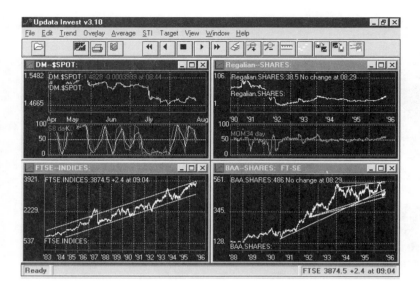

The Invest package above has been used to produce all the graphs and analysis in the first part of this book. This type of package is suitable for the investor who is not watching real time data.

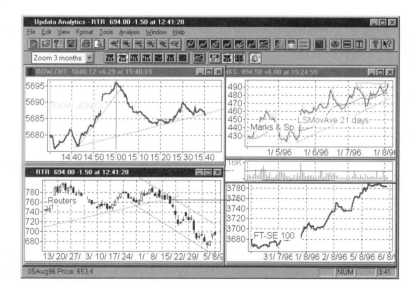

Analytics, on page 172 (bottom) is a package for real time graphing. This software is used for the next section on real time analysis. The top left window shows the Dow Jones index with every price change over a few hours and the bottom right window shows the FT-SE 100 index with every price change over a few days. In the next section, we see how the same techniques used on daily graphs can be utilised for the very short term.

Portfolio Management

Managing your portfolio can also be a bit of a chore. At Updata, we have always viewed this as secondary to using your PC to make more profitable decisions. It seems that the British investor is often more obsessed with counting his money than making it. A high proportion of investors use Quicken or a spreadsheet to manage their portfolios for tax purposes. If you are doing really well you may afford an accountant to do this once a year for you. You may also find your broker to be helpful here (see chapter on investment strategy). For higher end portfolio management, investors are faced with a choice between Fairshares and a new product from Updata called Portfolio.

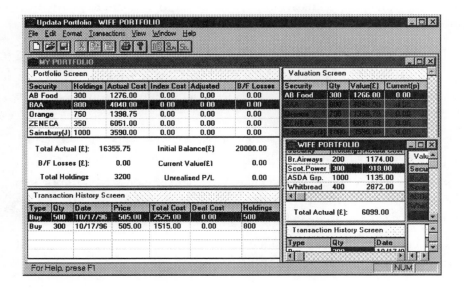

Portfolio lets you enter your transaction details and group a series of portfolios to give you the full bottom line, even in real time. It will also print out reports for capital gains tax as well as transaction summaries to help you evaluate where your most successful trading has been.

A few simple rules for purchasing investment software:

In *Profit from your PC* we provided a few simple rules to assist with purchasing investment software. Here we expand those rules taking some of the changes that have occurred in the market.

1. Has the company managed to keep up with the technology and what are its plans for the future? What is the company doing on the Internet?

2. What is the policy for upgrades, once you are on board? Are technical releases free and are upgrades heavily discounted?

3. Is there, somewhere you can see it, Trade Shows, Open Days, Shops, Demo Suite, Demo disks, or trial packages? Can you get a feel for the various products and their functions over the Internet?

4. Are there any hidden extras, like data or support fees? What happens if your PC is stolen or you wipe all your files?

5. What is the policy on technical support? What support is offered other than over the telephone?

6. What is the compatibility with other software packages?

7. Are there any press reviews available, third party endorsements, users etc.? Has the company carried out user surveys, can it provide you with a summary of the results?

8. Is there a user group, forum, newsletter, or place where users can meet? Does the company have a mechanism for putting you in touch with other users?

9. What is the product documentation like? Are there any on-screen tutorials to help you get to grips with it? Can the company offer you assistance beyond a user manual such as a guide to help you get more from the products?

10. Does the company have relationships with a number of stockbrokers? Can it provide details of brokers that are using it?

PART TWO

Getting More Advanced

'Information is power.'

GORDON GEKKO
(played by Michael Douglas) –
WALL STREET

CHAPTER TWELVE

Real time systems and analysis

Readers of *Profit from your PC* may have detected that I have often questioned the value of real time data (points for and against relative to investment strategy are covered in the next chapter). Having had a number of real time systems at my fingertips over the past year, I have to admit there are true benefits for the serious, active investor. If you are already spending a good deal of time in front of your system each day you should be considering moving up to real time.

Real time data services were covered in the last chapter. Here we take a brief look at the main elements of a real time system and how to interpret and analyse real time information.

Real Time Systems

The key elements of a real time system can be broken down into the following main elements:

1. Prices

2. News

3. Graphs

Prices

Price display screens have had thousands of spectators in the City over the years. Screens full of numbers can often be difficult to assimilate. The main ingredients are standard quote screens like a screen full of FT-SE 100 constituents with blue, red and green colour coding indicating rises, falls and no change respectively. As shown in the last chapter these screens can extend to viewing fields such as bid, ask, high, low, change, % change, volume, trades and time of update.

There is normally functionality to have custom quote screens and ticker windows where prices scroll from right to left. Ticker windows can also be customised, allowing you to focus on price changes that affect you.

Price screens are more suited to monitoring and dealing. Market analysis only really begins with features such as 'leaders and laggards'. Leaders and laggards in real time can become very interesting because you can watch shares rising and falling within the rankings list.

It also helps to show when a story has broken, which is not always that easy with straight prices and news screens. Once you see a price moving up a leaders list, you can access the news story or graph to find out more.

News

While the newspaper can serve as a useful digest for the market, it is always yesterday's news. Though this might be changing gradually with the Internet (see Part Three), people will read paper-based newspapers for some time. Even electronic papers won't give you the story as it breaks. There will be some delay in putting the content together.

Real time news services such as PC Market-Eye's news can offer a clear advantage in seeing the story break and watching the market react. I would recommend that you become very practised at this, if you are going to make this a major part of your investment strategy.

Don't forget thousands of professionals have been doing this every day for years, and remember a lot of them still don't get it right.

The PC Market-Eye news service is derived from the London Stock Exchange Regulatory News Service (RNS), which requires listed companies to report any information or announcements that may materially affect that company's share price.

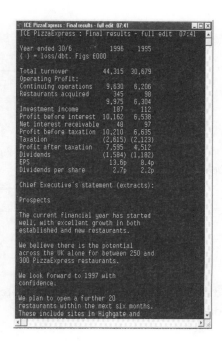

The PC Market-Eye screen on the left offers a list of stories, leading to more detail on the right. The market summary is useful and more up to date than those on the teletext services.

Graphs

Clearly this is the area I value the most. The rest of this chapter covers graphical analysis on real time data.

An intra-day graph, sometimes called a tick chart, is one that takes all the points within a day and plots them. Those using day charts with high/low bars may find the picture overleaf helpful.

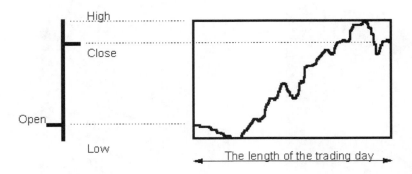

The daily bar in a normal graph is stretched to show the price movement within that day.

I used to be sceptical of carrying out analysis on real time intra-day graphs, but as I have watched them over the past couple of years it is clear that the same principles apply as with longer term daily graphs. With the FT-SE graph changing every minute over a nine-hour trading day, this graph becomes as detailed as a year and a half of daily data. Following intra-day graphs also serves as useful practice for understanding trends, breakouts and breakdowns, as they occur much more frequently. This means you can build your own knowledge base of how markets and shares behave more quickly.

Real time graphing is a capability available to most professional investors in the City. Increasingly Updata graphical analysis products are been used by this community. Serious private investors can take heart that the software they are using is as good as and often better than that at their broker's fingertips. If you don't believe me, try asking your broker next time you talk to him what the best performing FT-SE stock is on the day, week, month or year.

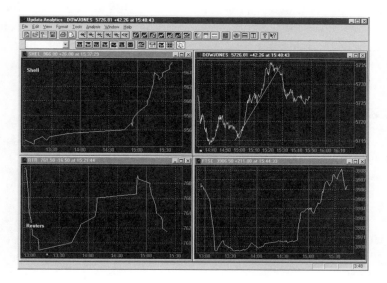

Source: Updata Analytics

Updata's Analytics program, above, running on the Bloomberg Open data feed. Updata's feed handling can utilise the Windows Dynamic Data Exchange (DDE) facility normally used for spreadsheets.

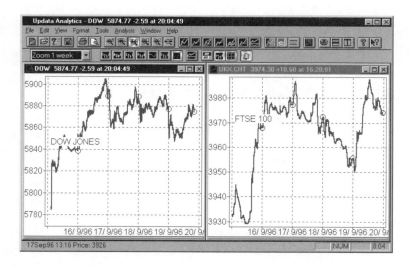

Source: Updata Analytics

The screen above ensures you can keep a close eye on the market. This shows weekly intra-day graphs of the Dow Jones index on the left and FT-SE 100 index on the right. The circles represent the end of each trading day. These graphs contain every price change in the market, over 2,500 data points, for the week. Being real time these graphs actually change right before your eyes.

Source: Updata Analytics

Building on the brief Dow Jones analysis in the introduction, we can progressively zoom in to see how the US market is moving around key levels on an intra-day basis.

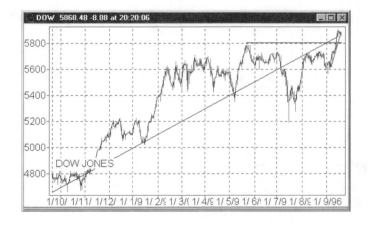

Source: Updata Analytics

The Dow has broken to an all time high for the first time in over four months. It was certainly very exciting watching this breach in real time.

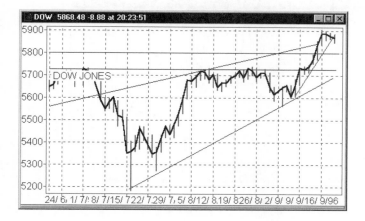

Source: Updata Analytics

This three month zoom shows how it broke the 5,740 level which had been a ceiling for some months and then moved quickly through the previous high at 5,800 a few days later.

Source: Updata Analytics

The two week intra-day graph above shows how the Dow soared through these critical 5,740 and 5,800 levels. Intra-day graphs highlight the technical nature of the market in the very short term like this.

Source: Updata Analytics

For the UK market, this graph over a week shows how the market goes through a constant series of fan shaped moves up and down. These fan lines can be drawn from peaks and troughs along the way. For short term traders, this helps to get a feel for reversals as they actually happen. Some of these short term peaks and troughs become highly significant in the longer term picture.

Source: Updata Analytics

Looking at the market a day later, the FT-SE 100 index really struggled to get through the psychologically important 4,000 level. This will be a key level for the

Footsie to test and will probably be dependent upon what the US market does over the coming days and weeks.

Source: Updata Analytics

Double checking the level of volume above shows how the recent rise has some weight behind it. The highest volume in the last few months was on the day the market broke through a key level of resistance.

Source: Updata Analytics

Looking at the market from a long term perspective, the trend channel shows it to be dangerously high. The higher it goes at this rate, the higher the risk of a dramatic correction.

Source: Updata Analytics

Tick charts are most useful for tracking market instruments that change frequently. The graph above shows a day in the life of the German Bund, the most heavily traded instrument (by volume) on the London International Financial Futures Exchange (LIFFE). This normally changes every few seconds, producing thousands of data points in a trading day.

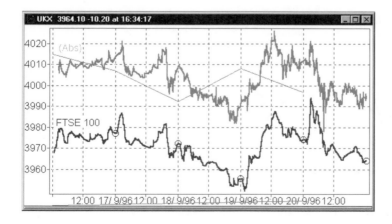

Source: Updata Analytics

The Footsie future is the most actively traded instrument (by number of trades) on the LIFFE exchange. The last graph shows the FT-SE future and the FT-SE cash (FT-100 index) ticking away on the same axis.

Naturally these graphs follow each other very closely. The future leads the cash market, such that serious investors often watch it instead of the Index. Many active private investors in the UK trade the FT-SE future. How some of them do it without a graph, I will never know.

Real Time Analysis of Stocks

Intra-day stock graphs are more difficult to analyse because the frequency of ticks (mid price changes) is more erratic. This in itself can be extremely helpful as you can see the busy periods before your eyes. It helps to highlight that 10% of time when prices are actually moving as illustrated below.

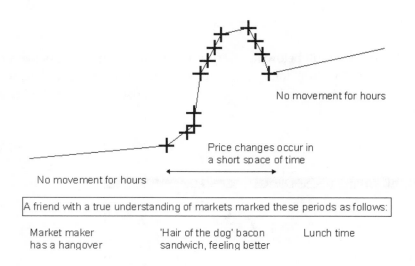

No movement for hours

Price changes occur in
a short space of time

No movement for hours

A friend with a true understanding of markets marked these periods as follows:

| Market maker has a hangover | 'Hair of the dog' bacon sandwich, feeling better | Lunch time |

Source: Updata Analytics

The graph below shows a sharp reaction in the Zeneca share price to bid rumours in the market.

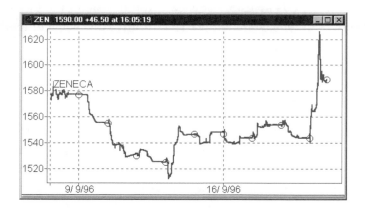

Source: Updata Analytics

Placing the ticks on the graph below helps to show where the dramatic periods of activity lie. The share price was fairly quiet around 10am and 3pm. The sharp fall between two ticks at 12:35pm off the back of the dramatic rise was the beginning of a consolidation.

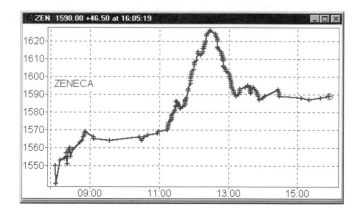

Source: Updata Analytics

Source: Updata Analytics

The longer term graph helps to put the day's change into context. Another big advantage of real time graphs is that the longer term picture always has the latest price on the end. Those relying on delayed data sources may not have the benefit of seeing this change on the graph on the day it happens.

The principles covered in Part One of this book can be applied to real time intra-day graphs, though the price differentials over minutes, hours and days may not be enough to trade profitably, after commissions, in many instances. The real advantage is watching events unfold as they happen. On finding buying opportunities, investors may view the cost of a real time system as a tool for getting in to a stock at a better price. For selling decisions, it may be seen as an insurance policy against getting out too late. This becomes increasingly true when markets are moving up as sharply as they have been recently with increasing scope for a sudden correction to the bottom of the trading range.

CHAPTER THIRTEEN

Routine and strategy

● ●

We covered routine in *Profit from your PC* to some extent and we categorised routine as follows:

Short Term Investor – Hold for Days, Weeks – Daily Routine
Medium Term Investor – Hold for Weeks, Months – Weekly Routine
Long Term – Hold for Months, Years – Monthly Routine

Routines normally get broken, but if you see a daily routine slipping to weekly, you need to recognise the time you are dedicating to watching the market and your investments might be insufficient for your intended strategy.

The two sides of the market

Before we look at routine and strategy I would like to take a quick look at professional investors and client-broker relationships. As I mentioned in the Preface, I have been amazed that a number of people have asked me to comment on more general aspects of investment. All I am doing is bringing together the two sides of the story that I hear. It is a bit like marriage counselling for clients and brokers.

At an institutional level the investment community is normally split into two categories known as the 'buy side' and the 'sell side'. These terms can be confusing for the private investor. For instance, fund managers would be classed as 'buy side' as they are the holders of stock, yet this community spends its life selling (sometimes hard-selling) its investment products direct to private individuals.

The 'sell side' encompasses brokers and market makers, who effectively spend their time selling to the 'buy side'. This process involves large dealing desks (maybe dozens of people), research departments and of course those long City lunches to assist the whole process.

For private investors buying shares directly, a similar analogy can be drawn. We are effectively the 'buy side' at this level and private client stockbrokers are the 'sell side'. Private investors account for less than one fifth of daily trading volume in the UK while in the US it is nearer half. While many professionals believe this is not set to change in the UK, I am certain that more and more people will wish to take control of their investments. The primary reasons for this are:

1. The rise of PC technology

2. Increased availability of information at a lower cost

3. Poor performance of managed funds

4. Growth of execution only services

5. Increase in home based working and early retirement

6. The rise in PEPs as an alternative to savings

As I started writing this book a revelation unfolded in the press that a highly regarded UK City institution had uncovered anomalies in the managing of some of its investment products sold to private individuals.

This activity related to trading activities of a star performer in the organisation. 'Nothing exceeds like success – so the collapse when it comes is devastating.' These trusts were bailed out by the company's German parent, but investors would have done better with their money elsewhere.

With the collapse of Barings, massive trading losses at Daiwa and Sumitomo banks and now this, many industry pundits are predicting that we may be seeing the tip of the iceberg.

Most financial regulators and large accountancy practices have had to build up teams of 'forensic accountants' in order to keep up with the ever more sophisticated webs of deceit that some City traders appear to be capable of. The bottom line is, can the City be trusted with our hard earned money? The more private investors I talk to, the more I uncover resentment of professionals who have managed their money.

You and your broker

The formation of The Association of Private Client Investment Managers and tockbrokers (APCIMS), based in London, came about as a result of the changes in the market in October 1986, known as Big Bang. While this organisation represents the interests of its member firms, it also looks after the best interests of private investors who are their members lifeblood. Most APCIMS members are authorised by the Securities and Investment Authority (SFA), who are widely recognised as having the highest standards of regulation in the investment industry. SFA members are subject to demanding capital adequacy tests and obliged to meet the most rigorous standards in terms of operating procedures and management controls, and only those individuals who are personally registered with the SFA are authorised to give investment advice.

Despite all these rigorous requirements, I still hear stories of investors losing a good deal of money when buying and selling shares. It is as if some brokers get their driver's licence and then at some later date decide to go joy-riding. Returns on stockmarket investments are never guaranteed, which is why the tools and principles covered in this book are designed to decrease the 'risk-reward' ratio dramatically in your favour. If you are buying and selling shares directly in the market you are going to have to accept responsibility for their performance. Don't forget that brokers are the 'sell side', though the better they perform the more client business they attract.

I have spent a good deal of time trying to understand how it can go badly wrong for private investors by talking to private client brokers. It seems the most common symptom is some clients have high expectations of very quick returns. This 'get rich quick' approach seems to be a number of people's undoing. The stories are like what you might expect to hear in a casino or a bookmakers. A man walks in with a few thousand and puts it all into one share in a small company or a short dated traded option and is angry to find he has lost a high proportion of his money a few weeks later. Investing is like gambling unless you minimise the risks with a system and a strategy. It seems people are mesmerised by the potential of quick returns. Double or nothing, red or black, pick the right number to win 35 times your money. In Britain every week, millions of people spend £1 or more on the national lottery for the chance to win millions of pounds. With odds of fourteen million to one, that's a lot of Saturdays. Most people forget about the odds and focus on what they will do with the winnings. They dream. Investors need to be realistic too. Brokers will tell you that some clients will not be told. Make sure you are not one of them.

Broking services normally fall into the following categories:

1. Discretionary

2. Advisory

3. Execution Only

Unless you are going to hand your money to a broker or independent financial adviser, you will be looking to choose between advisory and execution only.

Execution only services have become extremely popular in Britain and most readers will conclude, combined with strategies such as those outlined in this book, that is all they need. There is no doubt that execution only services have a good deal to offer, but this kind of service might not necessarily suit all active investors. Most of the successful private investors I have met have developed a good working relationship with an advisory broker.

Maximising your broker relationship

Advisory brokers normally cost a few pounds more on the commission, but can often well outweigh the additional expense in dealing at a better price and advising on timing. Stockbrokers are obliged to deal at the best price in the market on behalf of their clients. While this is comforting it can also be a barrier to a broker's bargaining on price. Execution only trades often go through very efficiently and quickly, leaving little scope for this. I have witnessed on screen shares quoted at a mid price with small trades occurring at a range of prices around this mid. The price saving can often seriously dwarf the commission saving if your broker works a little harder on your behalf.

The best business relationships are often built over a lunch or a drink. Investors need to view their trading as a business. Being a successful home based investor is a dream for many people, but it can be a lonely game. This loneliness can often extend to a level of anxiety which affects investment decisions. At Updata, we have found via our user group evenings and seminars that investors really enjoy meeting one another and exchanging ideas and experiences as well as phone numbers. I know investors who live hundreds of miles apart who discuss graphs with one another over the telephone.

Taking your broker out for a drink and a sandwich one lunchtime may be the best investment you could ever make. It seems that there is generally room for improved client-broker relationships. Rather than identifying the reasons for this, sensible investors will take the initiative to address this themselves. I remember, when I first started trading, a feeling of being a hassle to my broker. He was often short on the telephone and I got the impression that he thought he was doing me a great favour. Then one day someone else came on the line who sounded more approachable. I was a student in those days and had heard all about the cost of those long City lunches, so I suggested a drink the following evening.

The service I received and the pleasure of dealing with this broker after an evening of a few drinks in the pub was so vastly different. My broker and I actually looked forward to talking to one another. Moreover there was far less pressure on me to deal. Favourite customers are not always defined by the amount of money they spend.

Once you have built a rapport with your broker, you need to make him understand how you wish to operate and the lines of communication between you. I thoroughly recommend a fax machine for sharing information.

You need to view you and your broker as a bit of a team. For instance what happens when you go on a two-week holiday? What instructions do you leave your broker? Who decides what is the right level to sell at?

If your broker has a facility to use moving stop-losses, you should be able to instruct him to sell if it falls through the stop-loss level. This is better than setting a fixed limit. One way of providing an advisory broker with a degree of flexibility is to mark any written instruction 'with careful discretion'.

At Updata, we are exploring automated tools that link your PC trading system to send instructions to your broker. We believe the technology will provide many exciting possibilities.

The following check list may be useful:

Does your broker

1. Recognise your voice, are you on first name terms?

2. Ring you to keep you informed and without expecting you to deal?

3. Invite you to come and see him?

4. Reward your business with his best ideas?

5. Ring you with bad news, before you call him?

6. Send you a frequent newsletter?

7. Keep you in touch with investment books, tools and systems?

8. Advise you on PEPs and tax allowances?

Personal Equity Plans (PEPs)

PEPs allow investors in the UK to gain capital gains tax relief on their portfolio. Many people forget just how flexible these can be and head to the large banks or institutions for these products. You can invest up to £6,000 each year and a further £3,000 in a single company PEP (this only allows one share in the PEP). A few brokers provide Self Select PEPs allowing you to be flexible with the instruments you put in your general PEP. If you are an active investor you can effectively have a tax-free trading account which allows you to trade, pay in dividends and hold cash in the case of a single company PEP for up to 42 days.

PEPs are nominee accounts where the client doesn't hold the stock. They are like a trust. Money can be moved around in the PEP but can't be moved in and out and in again for the tax break. Many investors now realise that you can invest this allowance year on year and build a sizeable fund which can compound even further. You can't place traded options or warrants in a PEP but you can put investment trusts in which are ideal for novice investors. This is where a good broker becomes invaluable. There are some good deals about. You need to be sure that your PEP is flexible with no start-up or management fees. Dealing commissions and dividend collection fees are the most you should expect to pay.

Self-administered pensions also offer tax efficient investment possibilities which you may explore.

Short Term Investor –
Hold for Days, Weeks – Daily Routine

Categorising people is invariably dangerous and doing so for private investors is no exception. Investors may, however, find it useful to consider this before deciding to give up work and attempting to make a million in front of a screen.

If you are going to have a regular daily routine it will probably be governed by the level of information that you have, with real time prices being most likely. You may well sit in front of your screen all day or have some other work that allows you to keep an eye on the market. I find there are four periods that I like to look at – opening, before lunch, when Wall Street opens and before the close. If I was forced to look at the market once or twice a day it would be the last two times while both the US and the UK are open. This period gives a feel to how the London market's move so far on the day will be affected after 2.30pm and how it might open the following day before 4.30pm. I also like to check what the Dow Jones closed at after 9pm, just in case there has been a total meltdown in the US.

Clearly the real advantages of real time are that you don't need to phone a broker every time you need a price and you can watch prices live as they approach critical levels. For options and futures traders this level of information is a must.

If you can't afford a real time system you probably can't afford to be a short term investor. The main reason for this is that you need a fairly sizeable pool for the smaller shorter term returns. A correction of a few hundred points in the market might reduce your pool to a level that makes it difficult to gain the loss back. This is the chasing your tail syndrome that a lot of gamblers go through. They lose and then resort to progressively desperate levels to win back.

Traded options allow for following the market in both directions and there are a variety of strategies which are beyond the confines of this book. Whichever way you look at short term trading is extremely risky with a small amount of money and experience of markets. If you are short of both, don't even think about it. Learn as much as you can with a medium to long term strategy.

Another aspect of being a full time investor is that you can end up becoming chained to your system. You need to identify the critical times, maybe even set some alarms and also get your broker watching for you. It is then that you can sit down and put your mind to the market. The rest of the time you should be able to relax.

Medium Term Investor – Hold for Weeks, Months – Weekly Routine

On the information side you could use real time prices and involve yourself in the market as and when you wish, but you are more likely to use teletext or end of day services.

If you use an end of day service, this allows you to look at your graphs in the evening for the trading day that has just been. Otherwise you are likely to look at your graphs each morning. If you are at work this could extend through to the following evening. Another strategy is to invest in the top 400 stocks which are updated six times a day on the teletext services. At Updata our software is able to update continuously from both channels, increasing the number of shares to over 500.

While you might keep your eye on your investments each day or so, a medium term strategy should enable you to analyse your investments once a week or so.

Long Term – Hold for Months, Years – Monthly Routine

Many long term investors rely more heavily on fundamentals for their analysis. Long term investors may be happier to look at long term trending stocks or long term recoveries. With this strategy you will expect to ride out the short and medium term corrections, but will still need to be wary of long term breakdowns through the trend.

Whichever strategy you adopt it is quite difficult making the transition from one to another. It is even more difficult deciding from day one that you are going to make a full time business of trading. Here you need tools for analysis and practising to learn more in a shorter space of time.

PART THREE

The

Internet

> **‘I fear we have awakened a sleeping giant.’**
>
> **ADMIRAL YAMAMOTO**
> (after Japanese bombing of
> Pearl Harbor)
>
> **BILL GATES**
> (CEO Microsoft Corp.
> commenting on how Netscape
> had alerted Microsoft to the
> value of the Internet)

CHAPTER FOURTEEN

Internet overview

● ●

In *Profit from your PC* a year ago I was wondering whether committing a whole chapter to the Internet (the Net) for UK investors was being a bit bold. Now in this book, I have set aside this section and realise it would be easy to produce a complete book on the subject. This section already assumes a level of computer knowledge and some of the terms. You may wish to re-read the Internet Chapter in *Profit from your PC* first.

What has changed in a year

What hasn't changed in a year would be an easier subject, as the Net is in a constant state of flux. The battle for the desktop in personal computing has been replaced by the battle for the Internet. The stakes are high. Netscape, an Internet software company, came to the US Nasdaq market last year and was valued at $2 billion. An Internet browser is a software program which allows you to surf the web looking at information on the World Wide Web (www). The hype and potential of the Net is such that a company like Netscape with 70% of the Internet browser market and virtually no sales can be worth a fortune virtually overnight.

A debate raged in the computer industry. Would the browser actually become the operating system? Would Netscape Navigator ultimately replace Microsoft Windows? Now it looks as if the Internet browser will be a fully integrated part of the operating system.

Bill Gates, Microsoft's famous founder and chairman, has turned his whole workforce (including over 12,000 programmers) to throw everything they have at the Net. This showdown has led to increased functionality and capabilities in browser software. Better still, the quality of information that abounds on the Net and its visual appearance and layout have improved dramatically. We look at some Internet sites that are of interest for UK investors in the following chapters. Here we look at getting on the Net, electronic mail and the World Wide Web.

Getting on the Net

The main ingredients you need for getting on the Internet are a modem, for connecting your PC to the telephone, and an Internet Service Provider (ISP) who provides you with a connection to the Net. Modems have become inexpensive and are available from most computer dealers and mail order via the PC magazines. The speed to go for is 28,800 (28.8k), otherwise you will tear your hair out. Service providers can be located in Internet magazines which update the ratings all the time. It is well worth checking for price comparisons and performance. Some ISPs are slower than others.

The main criteria is that you can call your ISP on a local telephone call. Some have national networks offering you the nearest point of presence, others are local companies. At Updata, we help our customers get on the Internet all the time. We have built relationships with ISPs and we use our own web site for keeping our customers up to date with product information and answers to Frequently Asked Questions (FAQs) on our sales and help desks. Customers can Email us and download data for their software. We currently have an Updata user forum under development allowing our customers to communicate with one another.

Electronic Mail (Email)

This was the most popular use of the Net to start with. People could send messages to each other electronically anywhere in the world. Email has advantages over fax because you can attach files to it.

At Updata, we now download files to our printing or copying companies rather than sending them. For joint ventures in the US we download files and programs back and forth to one another, saving time and courier bills. Email can also be sent to a number of recipients simultaneously. A typical Email screen is shown opposite. Simply type in your message, address it and click send.

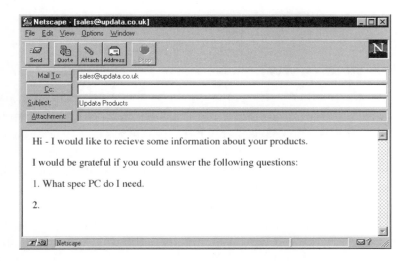

The most major problem with the Internet is bandwidth. To reduce this, data is invariably compressed or zipped by data compression software. This means the files are smaller and the time to download them is much less. The files are then unzipped at the other end.

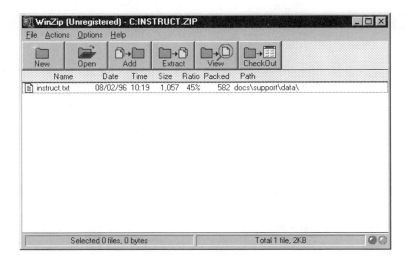

Instructions for collecting data from the Updata web are downloaded by clicking on them. They are zipped and once you have them you double click on this file and they automatically unzip and come up on your screen.

World Wide Web (www)

The real success of the Internet has been the growth of the World Wide Web. The Web has done for the Net what Windows did for computers. No more complex commands and key strokes. The Web is highly intuitive and interactive. Moving the mouse around in the browser, the pointer changes to a hand wherever there is a link to something else. This could be another web site which may reside anywhere in the world. All for the cost of a local phone call.

The browser below is the popular Netscape Navigator. Like most software programs, it has menus and a tool bar with a series of functions. Below this is a long horizontal window where you can type in the Internet address (Uniform Resource Locator – URL) for the site you wish to visit. The arrow on the far right allows you to access recently visited sites and you can 'bookmark' sites you wish to visit again in your browser. The nature of the Web is such, however, that I simply log on to the Updata site each day, click on the Internet Directory which opens up access to a whole series of sites, by clicking on these sites within the directory. We maintain our site directory with new sites as we find them. Other sites that we link to do the same, meaning that you will be presented with new locations all the time.

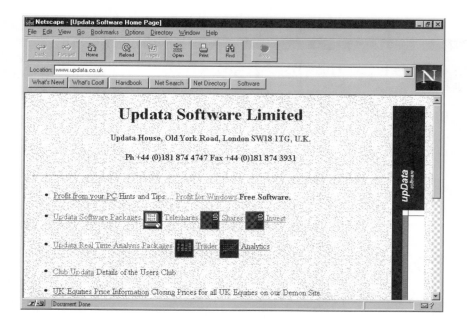

The Updata web site viewed through the Microsoft Internet Explorer – this browser allows different font types. Clicking on the logo on any Updata page takes you back to the Home Page. Or you can go back a page by clicking 'Back' on the browser tool bar. Another way to find information you want is to use a search engine. This lets you type in the key word you are looking for and you will be presented with a number of matches. You can then click on any of these that look interesting.

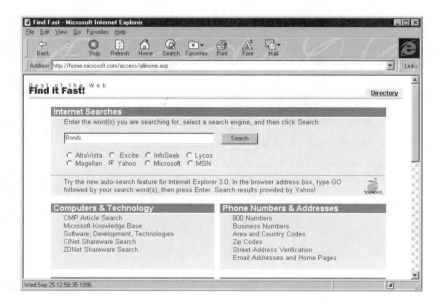

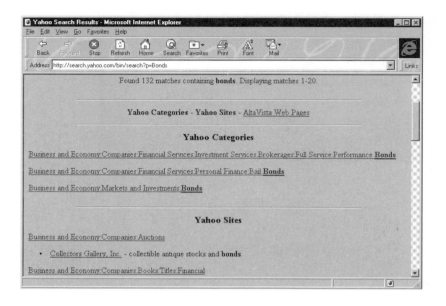

The search results are displayed with 132 matches found.

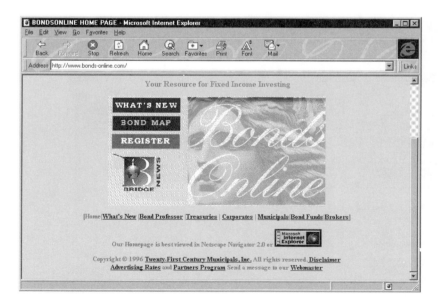

This is a new site that I have not visited before. Now I can decide to look at it or not.

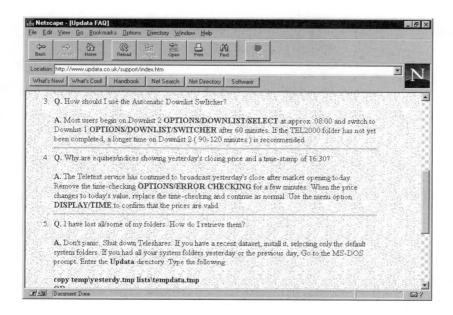

Frequently Asked Questions (FAQs) for technical support on the Updata help desk.

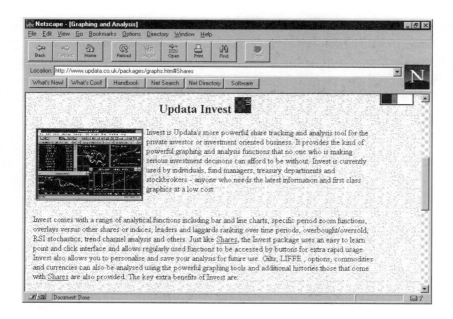

Product Information saves waiting for a brochure in the post and you can print it out.

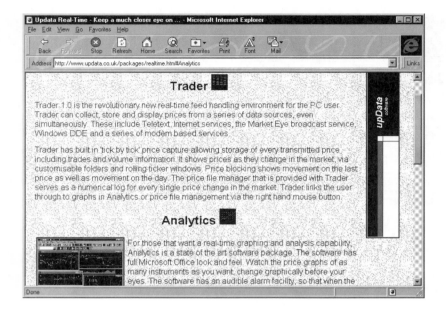

If you want to see how the software might look on your computer, click on the picture.

The browser gives a better feeling on screen for software than a brochure ever can.

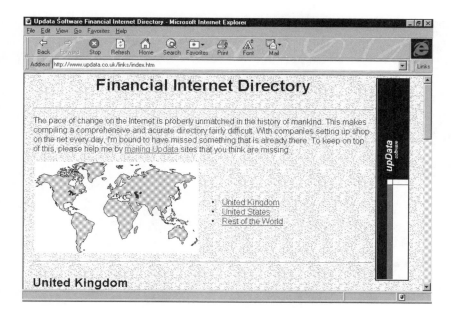

The directory of financial Internet sites lets you click on places on the world map.

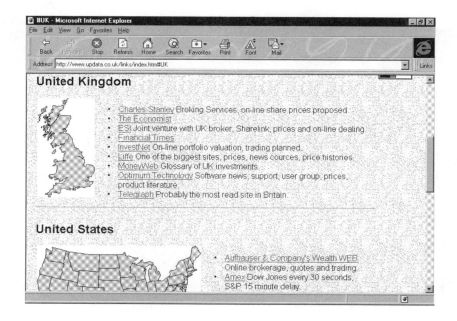

This takes you to the relevant country with a list of sites to access. The underlining indicates a link to another page or site. Simply click on it to go there.

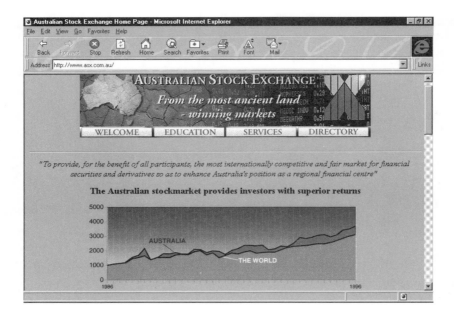

This is a favourite of mine from the rest of the world. Great for keeping up with the Australian market.

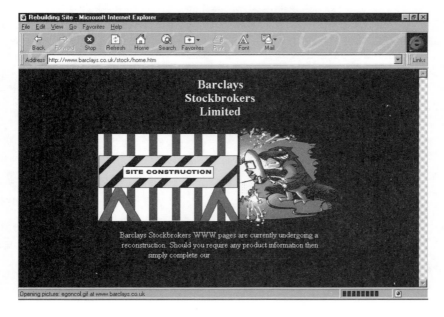

The Internet has roadworks all over the place. The welding griffin is animated here. It takes time to come up on screen, but is very clever. A site to look out for.

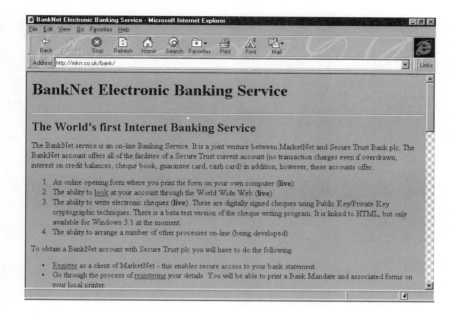

This site, above, shows the early signs of the potential of the Internet for on-line banking and other services. Home shopping is also set to be huge, along with buying and selling investments over the Internet.

CHAPTER FIFTEEN

Price information on the Internet

● ●

A year ago there weren't many companies putting price information on the Net. Now it is appearing on a number of sites with improved services being announced all the time.

Directories

In the US the Yahoo site (they also went public last year for more than $1 billion) serves as a hub. One of its specialities is financial information. This type of site is appearing in a number of places. One of the problems is the more comprehensive they become, the harder it gets to find things.

From the Updata Web site there is a link to the Moneyworld site, which is one of the best Internet directories for financial information in the UK. Updata's site is more for serious investors who don't want to look at Mortgages, Pensions, Insurance and Personal Finance. Moneyworld does cover everything though, so it is well worth keeping an eye on.

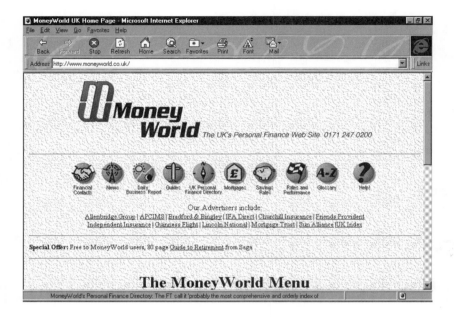

The Moneyworld site is one of the best places to start if you are looking for financial information on the Internet.

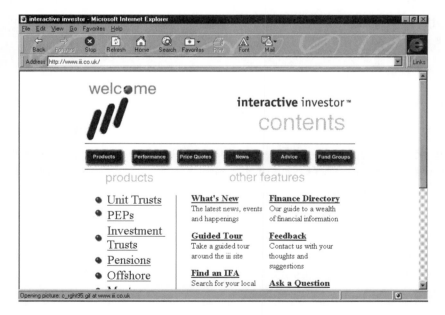

The interactive investor site is more targeted at investing than personal finance.

Information Providers

A number of information providers are starting to put information up on the Internet as well. Including the latest site with real time prices from Prestel On-line.

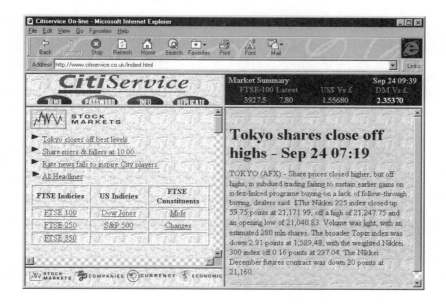

ESI, below, is one of the best known sites in the UK. It provides a host of facilities including live prices, news, on-line dealing to brokers and company information.

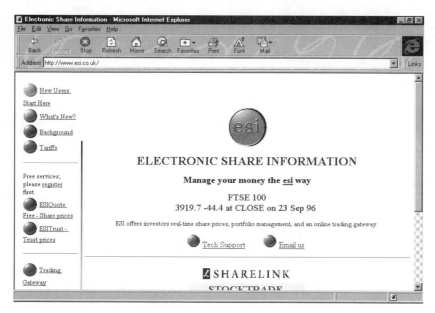

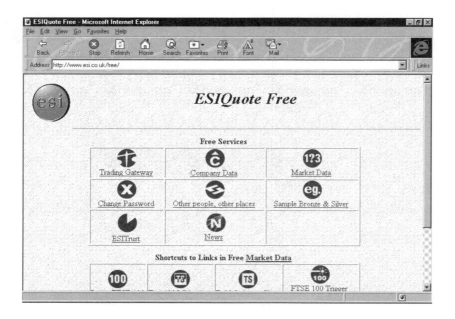

You need to register your name and address first. Some services are free and some are not. It is worth a good look around.

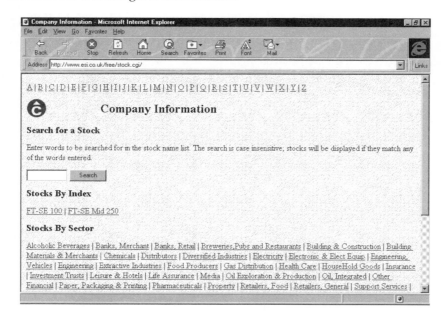

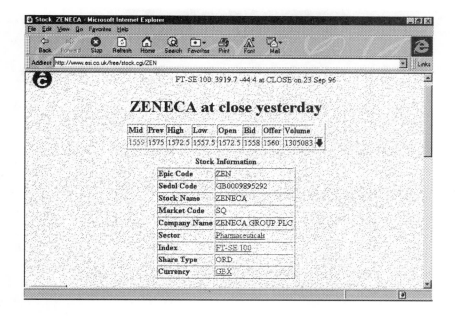

The last screens show how you access company information by entering the name of the stock you are interested in. You then get a summary as follows.

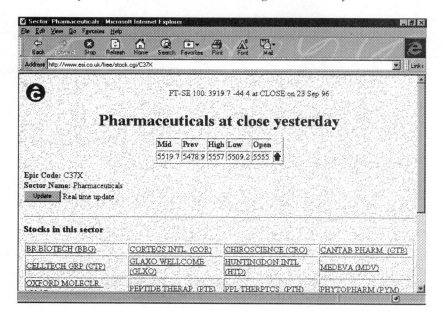

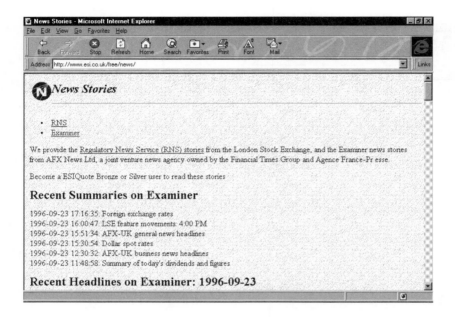

You can also look by sector and at relevant news stories.

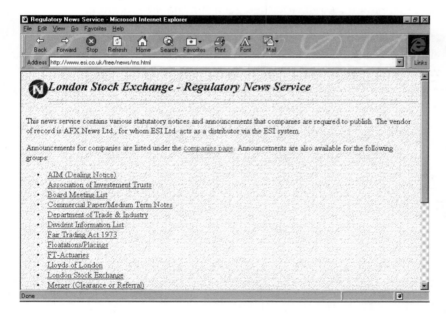

The news stories accessed by sector or other groupings relating to the story.

Exchanges

Some exchanges have been slow to put information up on the Internet for fear of undermining their business of providing data to the information providers.

The Australian stock exchange (picture in last chapter) and the US futures exchanges have been quick to respond to the demand for data by providing some excellent services over the Internet.

This information is not purely prices. News and market summaries as well as some interesting background information about each exchange are also provided. The LIFFE exchange in particular is providing historical data on a CD with the ability to update it thereafter via its Internet site.

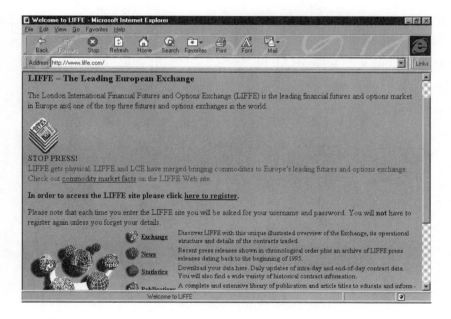

The LIFFE Home page.

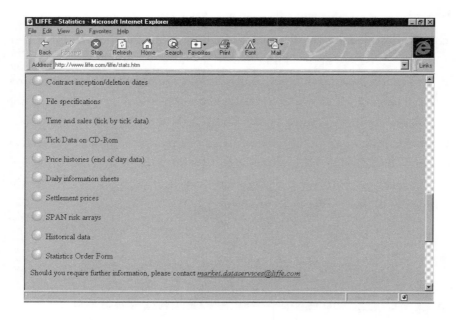

Access to the various data services LIFFE has started to provide, shown above.

"The more comprehensive the
Internet becomes, the harder it
gets to find things."

Newspapers

Newspaper publishers have really embraced the Net with the threats and opportunities that electronic publishing present. These sites offer price information services like those in the back of the newspaper and stories as well. The big advantage is that you can search archive editions for previous articles.

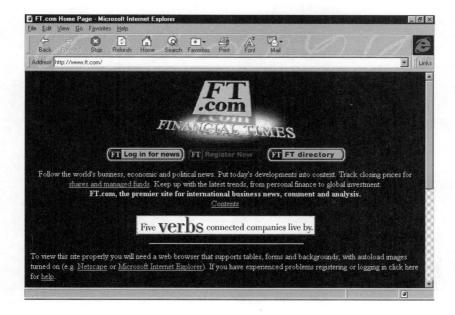

The FT site is naturally one of the best for investors. It is like the paper itself with some stories available to download or print. You are required to register your name and address but thereafter access is free and easy.

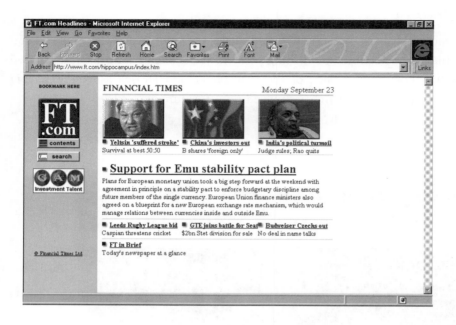

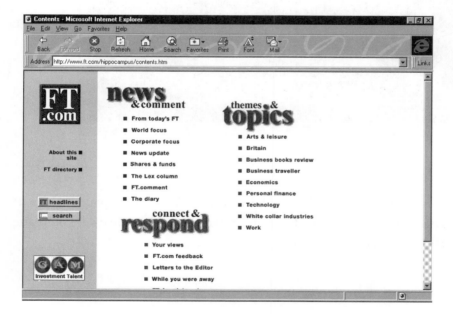

Pages of news headlines and contents are available leading you to the more in-depth information you may be seeking.

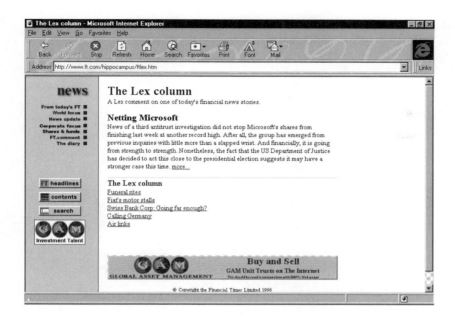

The Lex column (a favourite of mine) is available. I would love every related Lex column mention attached to my share graphs one day.

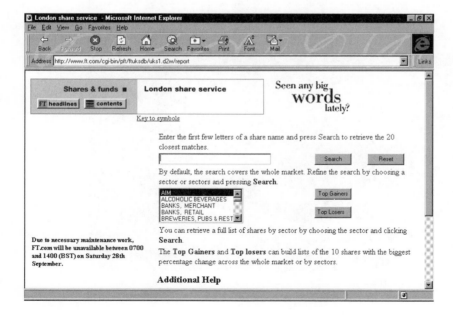

You can also access companies via a sector drop-down menu on this page.

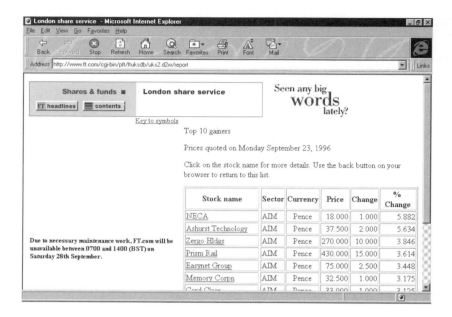

Having chosen the sector you can see a list of prices as you would in the paper.

The *Electronic Telegraph* is still one of the best and most visited sites in Britain.

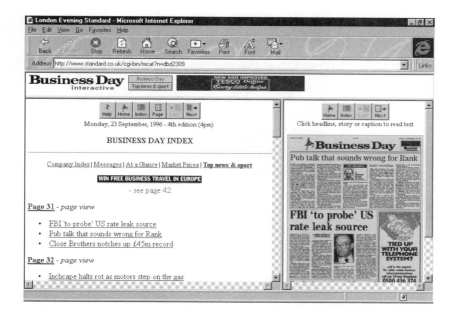

The *London Evening Standard* is also a great site which offers the full editions that you would normally receive in the City, only earlier. Great if you're not in London.

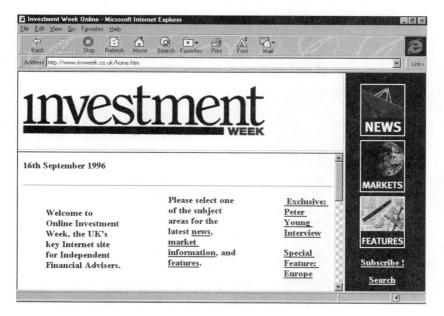

Investment Week gives you access to a weekly magazine normally only available to investment professionals.

Overseas

There are a number of sites overseas, especially in the US. A few good ones are:

Etrade by broker Charles Schwab in US is great.

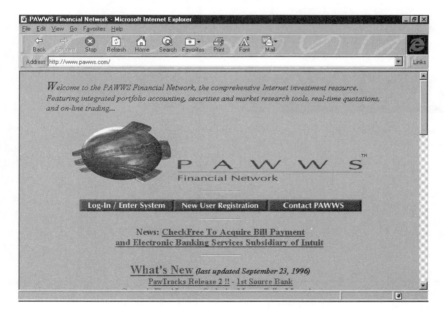

The Pawws financial network is also very comprehensive.

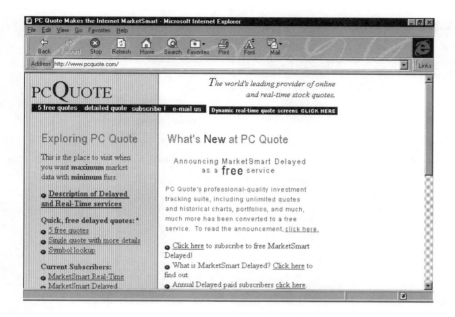

PC Quote also have a good site.

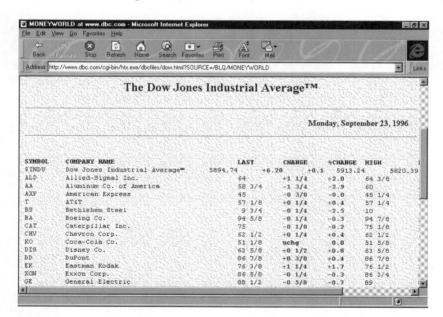

The DBC site is great for seeing which stocks in the Dow are driving the change in the market. One big company's price falling heavily here can send reverberations right through world markets.

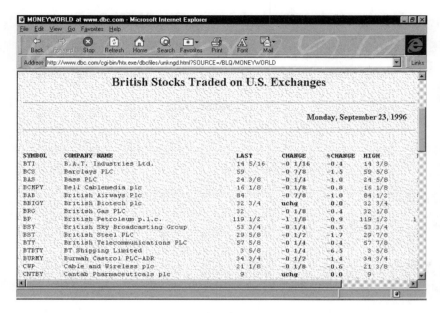

British Stocks Traded on U.S. Exchanges

Monday, September 23, 1996

SYMBOL	COMPANY NAME	LAST	CHANGE	%CHANGE	HIGH	
BTI	B.A.T. Industries Ltd.	14 5/16	-0 1/16	-0.4	14 3/8	
BCS	Barclays PLC	59	-0 7/8	-1.5	59 5/8	
BAS	Bass PLC	24 3/8	-0 1/4	-1.0	24 5/8	
BCMPY	Bell Cablemedia plc	16 1/8	-0 1/8	-0.8	16 1/8	
BAB	British Airways Plc	84	-0 7/8	-1.0	84 1/2	
BBIOY	British Biotech plc	32 3/4	uchg	0.0	32 3/4	
BRG	British Gas PLC	32	-0 1/8	-0.4	32 1/8	
BP	British Petroleum p.l.c.	119 1/2	-1 1/8	-0.9	119 1/2	1
BSY	British Sky Broadcasting Group	53 3/4	-0 1/4	-0.5	53 3/4	
BST	British Steel PLC	29 5/8	-0 1/2	-1.7	29 7/8	
BTY	British Telecommunications PLC	57 5/8	-0 1/4	-0.4	57 7/8	
BTBTY	BT Shipping Limited	3 5/8	-0 1/4	-6.5	3 5/8	
BURMY	Burmah Castrol PLC-ADR	34 3/4	-0 1/2	-1.4	34 3/4	
CWP	Cable and Wireless plc	21 1/8	-0 1/8	-0.6	21 3/8	
CNTBY	Cantab Pharmaceuticals plc	9	uchg	0.0	9	

Another fantastic feature of the DBC site is the ability to watch UK stocks, which trade on Wall Street, after the London market has closed.

CHAPTER SIXTEEN

Fundamentals data on the Internet

● ●

PC based investment has normally centred around prices on a screen or technical analysis. One of the most exciting areas on the Internet is the provision of fundamental data such as news, company accounts, brokers' forecasts and information about a company's business activities.

The Hemmington Scott UK Equities Direct site is the most comprehensive in the UK at the moment and a few screen shots of what you can get follow. Another site to look at is Corporate Reports (www.corpreports.co.uk).

> "The Internet bridges the gap
> between fundamentals and a
> technical approach for
> PC based investors."

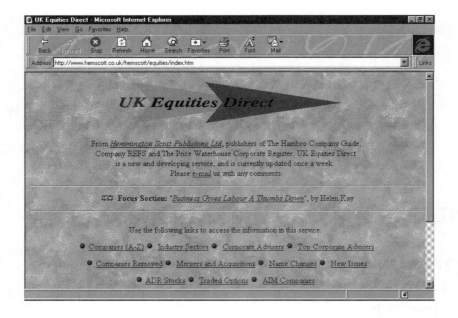

The UK Equities Direct Home Page is the main point of access to the information. If you have ever used any of Hemmington Scotts' publications such as the Hambro Company Guide you will be familiar with the type of information that this site covers. The guides are probably still more convenient to have at your fingertips, but this site is great if you just want the occasional piece of information about one company.

The other great advantage is that this site is being constantly updated, giving you recent results which may not have made it into the last guide you have received. Having heard Hemmington Scott's strategy first hand, I am sure this will become one of the most useful sites for private investors in the UK.

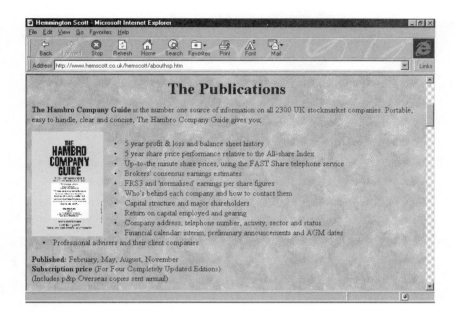

Product information is covered with a summary of what each guide offers.

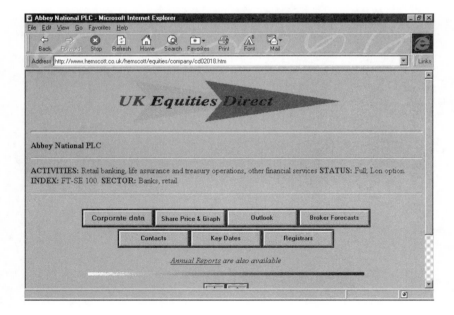

Having selected a stock, you can now access different types of information.

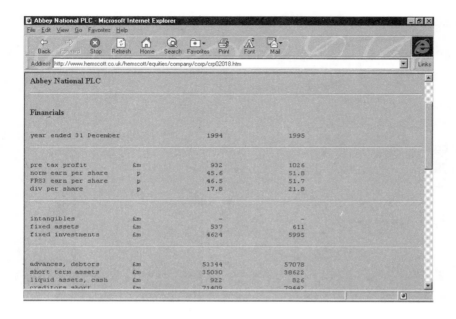

The company's accounts are available and can be printed for you to study.

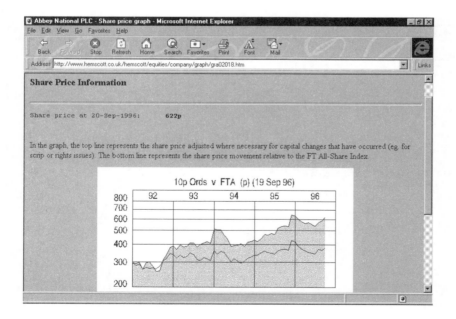

Very basic share price graphs are available as well.

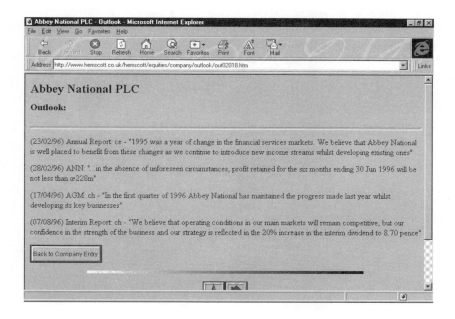

One of the most useful pages gives you the outlook for the company.

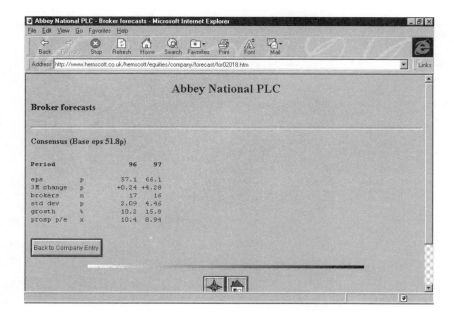

Consensus broker forecasts for the next results also help investors.

The Economist (the best magazine in the universe) offers great background long term fundamentals information and unbiased comment. Its web site is fabulous. It allows you to get articles you may have missed as well as accessing their statistics.

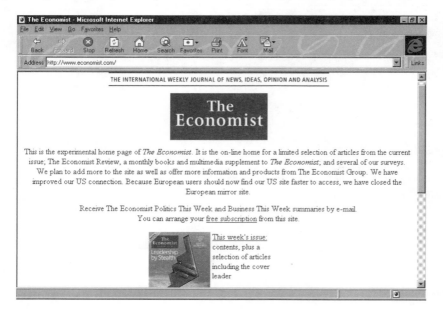

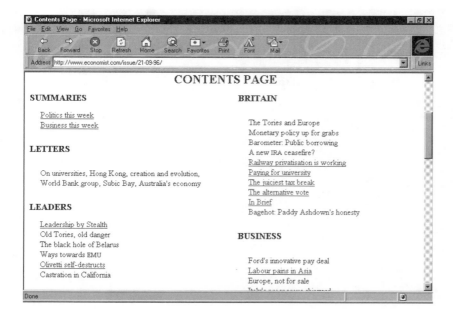

The contents page gives you access to the underlined articles.

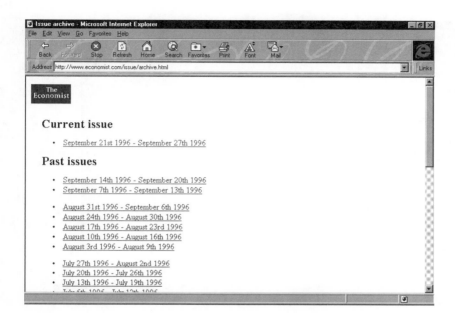

Here are the past issues if you missed them or would like the text of a story.

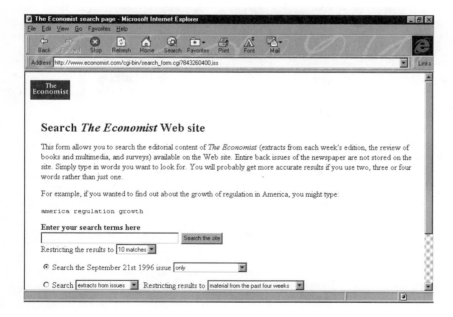

The Economist has also provided its own search engine. I looked up Dow Jones.

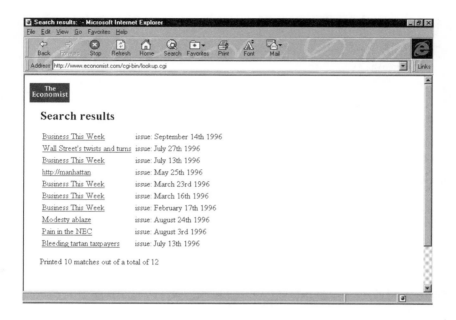

The article that I was after is the second one. I remember I didn't get to finish it.

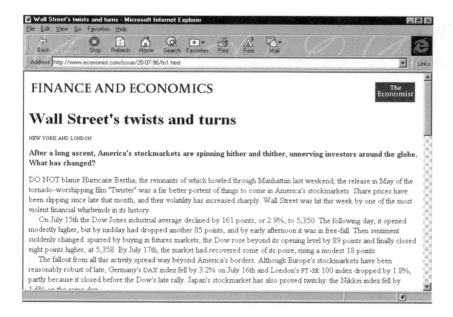

Here is the full text of the article which I printed out to take home and read.

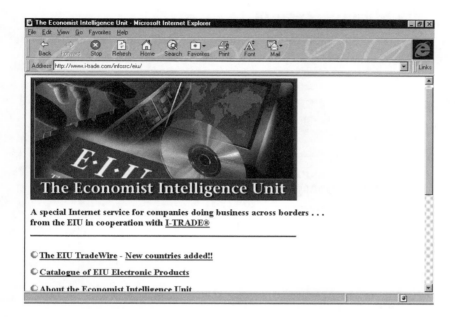

The Economist Intelligence unit is great for international business and investment.

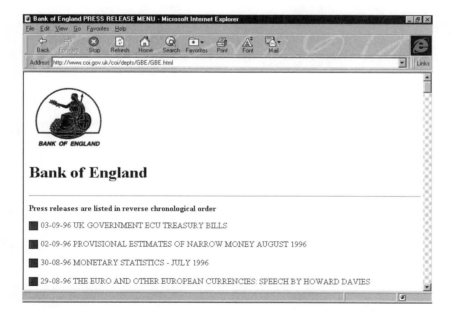

The Bank of England provide reports that investors may find interesting.

Brokers and On-line Dealing

Broker sites offer a range of information about products and services, but the market commentaries offered by some are excellent.

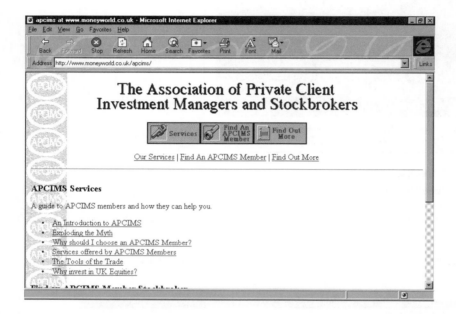

APCIMS (see Chapter 13) is a good place to source brokers.

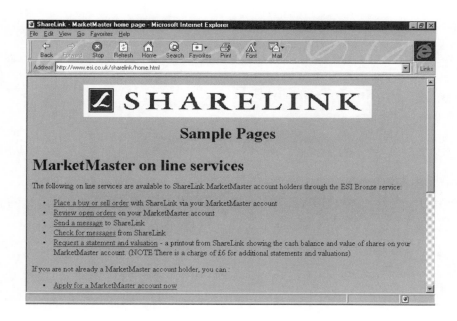

The Sharelink gateway for on-line placing of orders accessed via the ESI site.

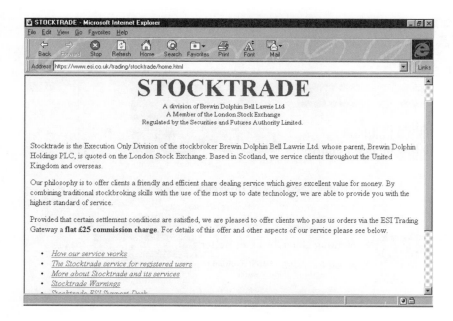

Brewin Dolpin's Stocktrade service is also accessed via ESI.

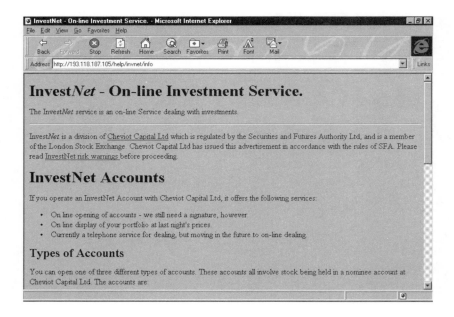

This Investnet service is poised to offer on-line dealing for PC users.

Fidelity have a high quality site with a range of pages.

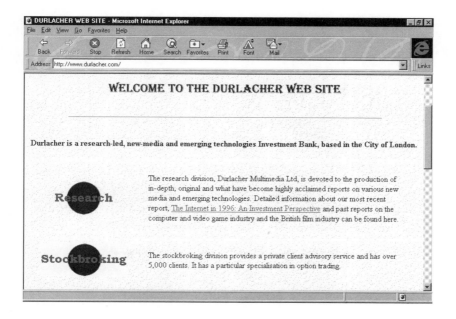

Durlacher's web site offers great research on technology trends and companies.

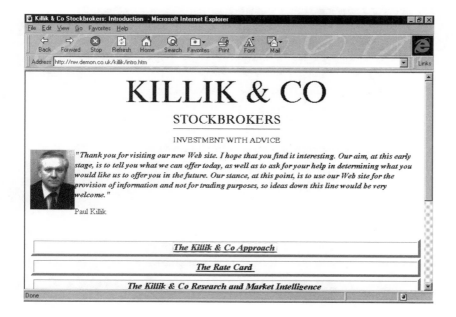

Killik's straightforward site is the best site I have seen for information on the market and companies. It really is great to see them putting their research out free.

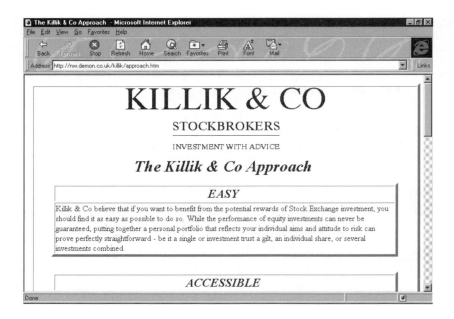

They also put across their approach and corporate culture very well.

The market report has grown out of a client fax service for all to see.

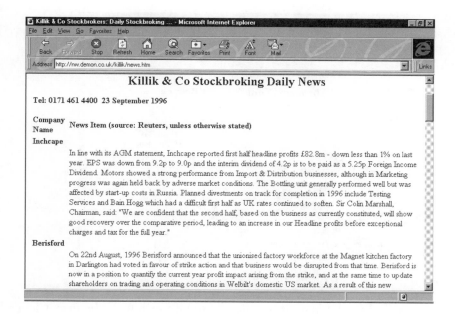

Killik & Co. give great summaries of results each day.

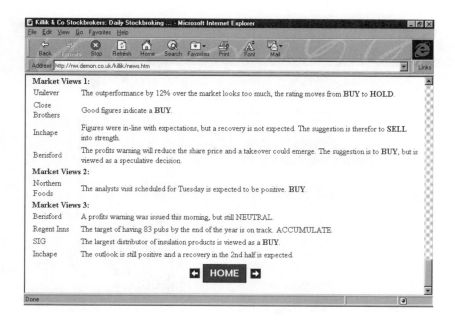

Killik are also the only brokers I have seen that are bold enough to put their trading recommendations on the site.

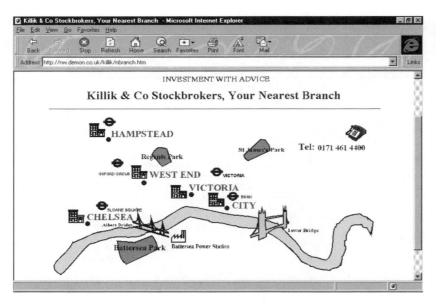

I couldn't resist including the map. It is a nice personal touch from the firm. Clever companies are making their web sites fun to use.

Other overseas sites

There are lots of overseas sites. The following two are ones that I have found interesting.

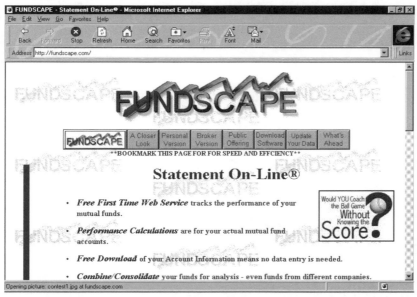

I love the 'would you coach the ball game without knowing the score' caption.

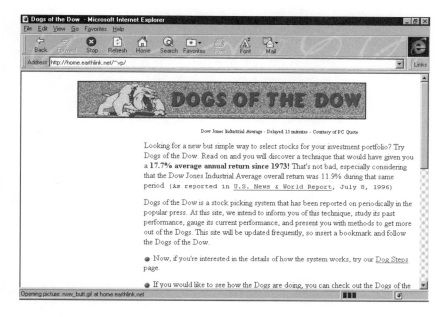

This 'Dogs of the Dow' site is also quite fun. Have a look sometime.

SUMMARY – A view of the future

The Technology

There are an increasing number of companies in the PC industry which are claiming to have a vision of the future. Vision implies some special gut feel for the way things are going. At Updata, we believe that this is a process better described as extrapolation, which in technology industries is non linear. The state of PC technology in two years' time is probably best judged by extrapolating from three years back to where we are now.

Three Years Ago

Standard Spec Machine:	286/386 – 16MHz, 4MB, 100 HDD
High Spec Machine:	486 DX – 33Mhz, 8MB, 200 HDD
Software	DOS 5, Windows 3.1 Launched
Internet	Small number of niche users
Modem	2400/4800 Baud
PC/TV	Unavailable
CD Rom	Announced

Early 1996

Standard Spec Machine:	Pentium – 90MHz, 8MB, 500 HDD
High Spec	Pentium Pro – 200Mhz, 16MB, 1000 HDD
Software	Windows 95/NT
Internet	Nearly 100m users
Modem	28,800/V34 Baud
PC/TV	Widely available
CD Rom	6 Speed – 650MB

Early 1998

Standard Spec Machine:	Pentium Pro – 300MHz, 32MB, 2000 HDD
High Spec	786 Chip – 300Mhz, 128MB, 5000 HDD
Software	Cairo (Full 32 bit object file system)
Internet	1 billion users, electronic commerce
Modem	100,000 Baud – cable or ISDN
PC/TV	Standard
Digital TV/ISDN	500 EC channels/ BT ISDN standard
CD Rom	24 Speed, Writeable – digital disks
Colour Laser Printing	1200 DPI standard

Poss. Low Spec boxes, software on demand via Internet

The 1998 view may be conservative. There will be aspects and capabilities that are even now difficult to comprehend. New main players will emerge whom nobody has yet heard of. Microsoft is likely to remain as the number one, but there will be applications that they will not develop. Investment software may well be one of them. The pressure to respond and include new features for our customers increases all the time. At Updata, we are starting to work on ideas that I would never have dreamed of. I used to say anything is possible in software. Now it seems truer than ever.

Implications for Investors

Active investors who are making their own decisions who don't embrace PC technology will find themselves increasingly at a disadvantage. The Internet looks like becoming as mainstream as the television. PCs in the home will become essential information points where you can do your shopping, book holidays or theatre tickets, see the weather in your area, search for information on a type of plant you are looking for, you name it. As Part 3 of this book shows, people will have a wealth of information at their fingertips. This technology will allow the home based investor to have information and software tools that approach those used by analysts in big institutions.

Software companies are now providing free programs on the Internet and money-back guarantees with their products. Large companies are starting to look at the private investor market. Order driven markets, where investors send out a message from their computer saying 'I have 1,000 BT shares to sell' and get back offers for their stock, will be soon upon us. The technology will allow investors to communicate with other investors and brokers on a mass scale. PC technology will become part of palmtop devices like organisers and mobile phones. You will be able to read a live market report while in a traffic jam or sitting in the garden.

It will all be rather daunting to begin with, but should offer some excitement as well. Among all of this the basic principles outlined in the first part of this book will be vital. All the technology in the world will not help investors who don't grasp the four rules. You will know them by now. If you don't, you had better go back to the beginning.

Appendix A
Internet Directory

● ●

All of the following web sites can be accessed from the Updata Software web site on:
    http:/www.updata.co.uk

AAA Investment Guide http://www.wisebuy.co.uk
    General Information on savings.

Abbey National http://www.abbeynational.co.uk
    Abbey National's offering to surfers with some financial information.

AFT http://www.hyperlink.com/aft/
    Applied Futures and Trading, Online magazine.

AIB http://www.aib.ie/aib/
    Allied Irish Bank's site with a great guide to derivatives.

Allenbridge Group http://www.moneyworld.co.uk/peptalk/
    PEP opportunities provided via Moneyworld.

Alternative Investment Market http://www.stockex.co.uk/aim/
    AIM – smaller companies with news and company information.

Altra Management Services http://www.textor.com/markets/altra/
   Foreign exchange newsletter.

APCIMS http://www.moneyworld.co.uk/apcims/
   Association of Private Client Investment Managers and Stockbrokers.

Applied Derivatives Trading http://www.adtrading.com
   Monthly derivatives publication with back issues on-line.

Bank of England http://www.coi.gov.uk/coi/depts/GBE/GBE.html
   Reports and releases issued by the BoE.

BankNet http://www.mkn.co.uk/bank/
   An Internet Banking service.

Barclays Stockbrokers http://www.barclays.co.uk/stock/home.htm
   Barclays Bank's share dealing service.

Cazenove http://www.cazenove.co.uk/cazenove
   Brokers services and information.

Charles Stanley & Co. Stockbrokers http://www.charles-stanley.co.uk
   An early web site which hasn't changed much.

Corporate Reports Ltd http://www.corpreports.co.uk
   UK Company Reports.

Currency Management Corp http://www.forex-cmc.co.uk
   Daily forex report and 24 hour trading.

Dogs of the Dow http://home.earthlink.net/~vp/
   A fun site with tips and 15 minute delayed prices and intra-day chart.

Durlacher Stockbrokers http://www.durlacher.com
   Private client brokers with good technology research.

Equities Direct http://www.hemscott.co.uk/equities/index.htm
   Hemmington Scott's fundamentals data, publishers of the Hambro
   Company guide.

ESI http://www.esi.co.uk/
On-line dealing and the FTSE in real time.

Fidelity Investments http://www.fid-intl.com/uk/home_e.html
UK on line investment centre.

Financial Information Network http://www.finetwork.com
Very comprehensive investor site.

Financial Times http://www.ft.com
The *Financial Times* web site – prices and news.

Flemings http://www.flemings.com
From the merchant bank with global information.

Forex Watch http://www.forex.co.uk
Foreign exchange, updated every 5 minutes.

FT-SE International http://www.ft-se.co.uk
FT-SE 100, FT-SE A All-Share and FT/S&P A World indices.

Global Asset Management http://www.ukinfo.gam.com/gam/indexmw.htm
International investment, funds and unit trusts.

IG Index http://www.londonmall.co.uk/ig_index
Financial bookmakers.

Interactive Investor http://www.iii.co.uk
Prices, news and advice.

International Finance and Commodities Institute http://finance.wat.ch/
Futures and options information – good source of information.

Investment Internet Journal http://www.discover.co.uk/~iij/
A fund managers regular summary.

Investment News Online http://www.ino.com
Prices, basic charts for global markets.

Investment Week http://www.invweek.co.uk
    The professional investment community's magazine.

InvestNet http://www.193.118.97.105/help/invest/info
    Offers various investment services.

Investor's Emporium http://www.pcquote-europe.co.uk
    Financial information from PC Quotes European office.

Killik & Co http://www.killik.co.uk
    One of the best broker sites around, well worth a regular visit.

LIFFE http://www.liffe.com
    London International Financial Futures Exchange.

London Commodity Exchange http://www.lce.co.uk/lce
    Now part of LIFFE, but the site is still separate.

London Evening Standard Business Day http://www.standard.co.uk
    One of the best newspaper sites, especially for financial pages.

Moneyweb http://www.demon.co.uk/moneyweb
    Personal finance.

Moneyworld http://www.moneyworld.co.uk
    The UK personal finance site – a great directory for investment.

NCB Stockbrokers http://www.ncb.ie
    Irish brokers with stockmarket information.

Ofex http://www.ofex.co.uk
    Unofficial Ofex (off exchange) dealing for high risk investment.

Optimum Teletext http://www.opt.com
    Teletext cards and software products.

Philip Alexander Securities and Futures http://www.bogo.co.uk/pasf
    Specialised information, especially futures.

Prestel Online http://www.prestel.co.uk/finance
New prices from Prestel – well worth a visit.

Redmayne-Bentley http://www.redmayne.co.uk/redmayne
Stockbrokers site with research.

Salomon Bros http://www.sbil.co.uk
US bank's global information.

Shareholder Action Handbook http://www.bath.ac.uk/Centres/Ethical/Share
Ethical investments and tacking action.

Small Company Investor http://www.aquarius.co.uk
Good background information for smaller companies.

The Economist http://www.economist.com
The Economist on-line, including back issues.

The Investor http://www.moneyworld.co.uk/investor
Proshare's magazine.

Trend Analysis Ltd http://www.trend-analysis.co.uk/index
Forex, metals, futures etc.

TrustNet http://www.trustnet.co.uk
Investment trusts information.

Tullett and Tokyo http://www.tullet.co.uk
Forex and derivatives.

WebFinance http://nestegg.iddis.com/webfinance
From Investment Dealers' Digest in the US.

Wolff Daily Metal Report http://www.rwolff.com
LME Base and Precious Metals.

◆

Appendix B
Summary of *Profit from your PC* Reader Survey

Have you referred back to *Profit from your PC* since first reading it?

☐ No = 5 %

☐ Once = 0

☐ A few times = 57 %

☐ Frequently = 33 %

How would you rate *Profit from your PC* alongside other investment books?

☐ Best I've read = 17 %

☐ Among the best = 62 %

☐ Average = 19 %

☐ Poor = 0

Has the book helped you with your investments?

☐ A vast improvement = 7 %

☐ Significant = 36 %

☐ A little = 48 %

☐ Not at all = 5 %

Have you used the book in conjunction with any software?

☐ Profit = 29 %

☐ Teleshares = 17 %

☐ Shares = 14 %

☐ Invest = 19 %

☐ Trader = 2 %

☐ Analytics = 0

☐ Other = 19 %

How powerful a combination have you found the book and software?
(If applicable)

☐ Extremely powerful = 17 %

☐ Good = 40 %

☐ Average = 12 %

☐ Not at all = 5 %

Which section did you like most?

The whole book

Chapter 8 – Practice Makes Perfect Profit

Chapter 6 – Basic Technical Analysis

Chapter 9 – Finding Stocks to buy

Using your system

Using technical indicators

Chapter 11 – When to Sell

Explanation of market movements

Graphing

Chapters 9 to 12

Part 1 – Getting your system in place

Trends and stop-losses

What did you see as the single biggest message?

1) Cut Losses 2) Cut Losses 3) Cut Losses 4) Let Profits Run

Cut Losses

Careful chart analysis

Cut Losses x 3

Early bird catches the worm

Stop-loss

You need a PC

It is not so difficult after all

Using stop-loss to cut losses

Being methodical and avoiding sentiment

Timing. Not buying too soon on tips and taking profits

Charts are a powerful investment tool

Technical analysis works

Investing should be pragmatic not emotional

Don't consider buying a share without a graph

Establishing a routine

Which parts, if any, did you not understand?

None

Getting more sophisticated was a bit hard going

Getting more sophisticated needs expansion – signals relative to charts

DDE Linking into spreadsheets

Identifying cycles, overlays rebased versus relative

Finding the right period

Some graphs were too long for the active investor

Using Technical indicators

What areas would you like to see expanded in a new title that follows on from *Profit from your PC*?

More on Relative strength to indexes

Traded options pricing

Section on dealing and choosing a broker – nominee accounts

Further chart analysis

Cycle periods

Some practical examples for moving averages and short term indicators

More detail on technical analysis

Trading systems

Obtaining data via modem

Accounts, spreadsheets, volumes

Alternative data sources

Collecting and Analysing Option prices

Hardware software and datafeeds

Real time data sources

Reducing the myth that you have to be a professional to be successful

Do's and don'ts of dealing with a stockbroker

Forward projection of cycles

Using technical indicators

Identifying cycles, overlays rebased versus relative

Expanded getting more sophisticated

How to choose moving average and STI periods

More on practical difficulties of using investment software

AIM market, bed and breakfasting and self-managed PEPs

When to buy, using examples without the benefit of hindsight

More examples of Buy indicators and how they worked

Advice on percentages to use on stop-losses

Choosing the correct part of the graph for analysis

Getting International data and the Internet

Testimonials:

'Profit from your PC'– book

"Having read your excellent book several more times, I hope that you won't mind my writing to you for a second time. I have read very many books and articles on charting over the years but none come anywhere near yours for clarity and reasoning."

Mr P Hood, Norfolk

"It covers the whole subject of charting in good depth whilst being easy for a novice like myself to understand." Mr R Davis, Oxon

"A very understandable read – should be kept close to your PC." Mr R Lines, Coventry

"Thank you for such a good book."   Mr J Wood, Preston

"The only book I have read which introduces the private investor to the profit-making link between the home computer and investment, without blinding or frustrating him with computer or investment 'techtalk'."   Mr J Oades, Middlesex

"Very readable with lots of useful information."   Mr P Mitchell, London

"I have returned to it many times and will continue to do so."   Mr R Shorer, Leics

"Linton's extensive study of technical indicators is an ideal basis for the part-time investor to use for buying and selling stocks profitably."   Mr Davis, Wantage

"This book cuts through the confusing mass of Technical Analysis tools and their conflicting messages to focus on what works and how anyone can profit from it. I have adopted the book and software that go with it as my investment method. What more can I say?"

Mr D Wilkinson

"A very good read, suitable for both the beginner and serious investor."   Mr D Hilling

"An easy to read and understandable book on what can be a very dry subject."   Mr P Mitchell

"As a very satisfied Updata Invest user, I find it difficult to suggest any areas of expansion. A real aid to the intelligent investor."   W Bramley

"I found this to be a clearly written approach to the subject."   P Cochrane

"Just what I was looking for!"   Mr M Cinover

*"I was considering buying a PC when I obtained a copy of your book **Profit from your PC**. If I had any doubts about buying a system, **Profit from your PC** convinced me I needed a computer. I did buy a PC and now I cannot live without it."*   Mr J Stacey

"I now feel it is safe to deal in stocks and shares."   J Otter

"Excellent Book and Read. Message came through very well and easily understood."

F Cowlishaw

"A superb introduction to share investment using a PC."　　　　　　　R Bryans

"A very well written and understandable aide-memoir."　　　　　　　B Hester

"The book and software has increased my awareness and interest in the Stock Exchange, to improve my portfolio performance."　　　　　　　A Hackman

"I have read **Profit from your PC** *and gone on to use your shares package. Both are excellent and at a very reasonable price."*　　　　　　　Mr G Selby, Somerset

"One of the most readable and easy to understand investment books I have read."
　　　　　　　Mr D Coomer

"I am most impressed with your programs. They perform excellently."
　　　　　　　Mr C Prior, Somerset

"The program works splendidly."　　　　　　　Mr Bradley, Maidenhead

"Since becoming a user of Updata software I now feel that I am in charge of my portfolio and have an investment strategy. I know when to sell."　　　　　　　Mr R Constant, Kent

"Superb value for money."　　　　　　　Mr D Farmer

" I would like to add that my system works well and is very reliable. I am often away from home and I rely on Teleshares to gather data in a totally unattended mode. It never fails. I would recommend your products to anyone."　　　　　　　Mr P Gannon, Warwicks

"If **Profit from your PC** *had been available when I started investing in the stockmarket, I would have saved myself from some very expensive mistakes."*　　　　　　　Jim Scaife

"A thoroughly enjoyable and informative book."　　　　　　　A Averill

"Very well written and not too much to take in. Worth while for either the novice or expert."
　　　　　　　Mr Thomas, Poole

"This must be the easiest read I have ever seen on chart analysis."　　　　　　　Paul Berry

"Graphs are clear and on the page referred to."　　　　　　　L Phillips

"I found it an excellent book, very informative, very well written and presented. I am looking forward to the next book."   Mr B Hill

"Other titles I have read on the subject have been very tedious."   S Hopkins

"A very useful and informative material worth digesting and applying to investments."   Charles Quaye

"A very understandable and digestible read, should be kept close to your PC."   Richard Lines

"A most informative manual."   Roy Compton

"I have been looking for a book like this for over 20 years, this is better than I thought possible."   Peter Goodin

"If you only have time to read one book on investment, this is the one."   R Smith

*"I feel happy with my book, **Profit from your PC**.*   Luis Eduardo Gaviria V, Medellin, Colombia

Many thanks to all those who took the trouble to fill out the survey, and providing me with invaluable feedback. I have been flattered by so many kind comments.

David Linton, October 1996

INDEX

Profit
for Windows
VERSION 2

Profit, Updata's stockmarket simulation game, is free to all ***More Profit from your PC*** readers.

Simply send this voucher, with your name, postal address and daytime telephone number to:

Updata Software Ltd
Updata House
Old York Road
London
SW18 1TG

Fax 0181 874 3931

Please forward My Free Copy of ***Updata Profit for Windows***, worth £9.99 to:

Name

Address

Postcode   Telephone